Small & Supercharged

Small & Supercharged™

Small Steps to Supercharge Your Brand on a Budget

Contents

1. Introduction

I love a motivational saying as much as the next person obsessed with motivational sayings, and if I could give you one, just one, as you embark on this adventure with me, it would be 'you've got this'. Because you have.

For years and years public relations (PR) and marketing has been seen as a dark art. It's not always what you know, it's who you know, right? Well, I'll level with you and say that knowing the right people helps, but when I started out, I didn't know any of the right people. So, I got to know them. One at a time. Whether it's getting to know the right people, learning new things, and trying your hand at new ideas and techniques to help you and your business, you can. Just do them one at a time, OK? The other thing that has to be mentioned is that the old 'rules' don't apply to everything anymore. We have social media and so much more to help you on your way.

But don't worry – we're in this together.

I've been learning, doing, trying and testing this stuff for years. I mean, over a decade, and I can promise you that nothing I do is magical. Well, definitely not on a Harry Potter scale. There have been lots of magical moments along the way, but I assure you that every single thing you read in this book is actually very logical and very easy to replicate. This is why I'm so excited to share it with you.

I want you, yes, YOU, to promote your brand better, whether you're a business or a personal brand. Because when we hide our sparkle from the world, whatever form that sparkle may take, we're not only doing ourselves a disservice, but we're not helping others either. Maybe you have the perfect product for someone who has been struggling with a very specific issue?

Maybe you're offering a service that will rock someone's world? Maybe your blog will change someone's life (yes, we're going that big here!) or make dark days brighter for them?

Who are you to deny them of that opportunity?

When you've been working your backside off, who are you to deny yourself the opportunity to get it out there into the world? Seriously? Whatever your gift, passion, product or service is, you NEED to tell people about it.

I can't guarantee that everyone will like what you do. But do you want to know the secret? You don't need them to. Through the techniques and tried and tested ideas in this book, you will be able to position yourself better and thus, attract your 'tribe'. I feel like tribe is such an overused word these days, but whatever you call it, that's what we're aiming for in everything. You don't want to attract people who have zero interest in you because if they don't get you or what you do, they'll never benefit from what you have to offer. You, in turn, will never benefit from them – I don't just mean on a monetary level. I mean at all.

But when your tribe finds you – the game changes. You have people who understand and support you, and if you have these people, this tribe of flag-waving cheerleaders, then you're on the right track.

So, don't stress about the 7.6 billion people in the world. Or the over 2 billion that use Facebook each month. Or the tens or hundreds of thousands who read the magazines you want to be featured in. Don't stress about it all. Think about who you want to attract and look at building your tribe and telling the right people what you do, one at a time.

Doesn't seem quite so bad now, does it?

Now, another thing I want to make clear is that I'm – how

should I put this – thrifty? Tight?! By which I mean that spending vast quantities of money isn't my thing. This has passed into the work I do too. Even when I have had substantial advertising budgets to allocate, I haven't actually enjoyed spending the money – and I've questioned every pound I've spent – I mean, will we see the return on our investment? Can we even track it? I know this sounds like an odd statement, but depending on the campaign, the business structure and so many other factors you often can't track the success of print advertising. What if I spend the money, that hard earned money, on the wrong thing? So, I focused on how I could get better coverage for less money and it worked really well. And continues to. It's a strategy that is easy to replicate. In fact, I've replicated elements of what you're going to learn for everyone I've ever worked for.

Start-ups often have non-existent marketing budgets – I know that – and often marketing is an area that gets cut when belts need to get tightened – and I get that too. Marketers (although I prefer the term marketeers!) aren't always seen as 'essential' to the business, by which I mean we don't often take the sales calls or pick and pack the deliveries. We don't always have a lot to do with product design or ordering. But without marketing, your product will remain a well-kept secret. Which means that your sales team could well be twiddling their thumbs, your pickers and packers won't be doing a whole lot and your product will remain in the warehouse. Just waiting. Patiently.

I am absolutely not telling you to spend the national debt on advertising or marketing. I'm not even telling you to hire a PR or marketing person. I'm not telling you to work with a freelancer. If your budget is small or you just want to try your hand at being a whole lot more creative with your marketing, you can still do really well. If your advertising budget is zero – you know what – that's when it gets exciting. Because if you have zero to spend on advertising but you have time and a product or service you need to sell and get in front of people, you're going to have to get creative.

I'm also not saying you should never spend a penny on advertising or sponsorship. By using the methods and systems I'm going to share in this book, you can do amazing things and get the word out for very little. This gives you more freedom to spend money in areas you know will make a difference.

Are you scared because you're in this predicament or excited about the opportunity that lies before you? Say it's the latter for me, will you? Because I'm very excited to be sharing all the things you need to help you promote your business like a pro, even on a shoestring. Actually, for nothing if you like. And I'm excited for you to feel the buzz of it all. I know it might sound far-fetched, but you will know exactly what I mean when it happens!

As you move through these pages, I really don't want you to feel overwhelmed. There are a lot of things you can do to promote your business for free, but it's likely you'll favour some over others. And that's fine if they work for your business. You don't need to be everywhere and, actually, your target client will favour specific areas too, which you'll find through research, trial, error and just simply asking questions, learning, watching and listening.

Let's go.

It would be amazing to connect over this book on Facebook, and as such please see this as a very warm invitation to join my Small & Supercharged™ Facebook group.

2. Believe in Yourself

Believe in yourself – because you're going to need to.

Let's explore a little mindset.

Mindset is such a key part of any brand. Most definitely in the promotion of any brand. Honestly. Because if you don't believe in yourself, your service or the product you're selling and wanting people to engage with, why would anyone else?

Of course, if you don't believe in yourself/brand/blog/product or service, you probably won't even bother to tell anyone that it exists.

And it will fail.

Can I tell you something else? Your brain won't tell you it's because you didn't do x, y or z. Most brains will tell you that you failed because you're rubbish. Your product/service/blog is crap – I mean, who are you to be doing this? You don't know what you're doing. [Insert name] said you couldn't do it/that you were mad/didn't know what you were doing and damn me they were right.

So, you're a failure, aren't you? A big old failure that should play safe all the time. Follow the 'norm' and never dream, because you're not made for big things. You're made to be average. You tried and you failed. You're embarrassed – I mean what will people think? You will never try again. Actually, it's probably better to try to find a rock to hide under.

I've laboured the point, but do you see where I am coming from here?

The fear of perceived failure can stop us doing so much. For me, it doesn't often stop me doing something. But it tries very hard to stop me telling anyone about it. I literally have to think 'if I was a client, what would I tell me?' Without fail it's 'come on, it's great, why don't we tell some people and see what happens before we start this cycle of feeling crap?'

Failure is a myth

The first thing I want to address is the idea of failure. It's kind of a myth. Did you know that without 'failure' we wouldn't have a lot of the things we know, love, and use every day?

There's many a great quote that states words along the lines of 'if you don't win, you learn'. And I really, really want you to think about this. If we think about everything we do as a learning experience and make it a whole lot less black and white, it gets easier.

Whatever you do in your life and in your business, it's likely you could improve it. But the more cycles of 'plan, do, review' we do, the better the thing we do becomes. As you move through this book, you'll feel the fear when you try something for the first time... because what if it's rubbish and everyone laughs/thinks you're stupid? I have a few things to say on this.

1. Your first attempt will not be amazing – well you won't think it is. That's just the way it is. But when you've done it once and put it out there, you can then review it and improve it. You cannot review something that doesn't exist.
2. Keeping something away from the world because it might not be perfect isn't a whole lot of use. And actually, it can waste a lot of time. When you read, re-read, redo, read, re-read and redo over and over again, you're wasting a whole

lot of time that you could use better. You could use the time to grow your business or just enjoy yourself, for example. There is a point – and I urge you to find systems that help you get to this point as quickly as you can – where you say 'yep, that's good, let's go'.

This isn't an excuse for shoddy work. It will allow you to grow and develop faster without beating yourself up, procrastinating and becoming stagnant.

Take a press release for example. You'll always spot the typo (if there is one) after you press send. It is just life. So do your best to avoid this. One thing I do is write on one day and review the next as my brain seems to be more able to spot issues when it hasn't been staring at something for ages. Some people use grammar software to help spot errors. Others get a friend or family member to check over important things to spot the typos. There are systems you can put in place to help increase your confidence and reduce the likelihood of a mistake.

1. You will make mistakes and you will do things you're going to really kick yourself for – we all do as we are flawed humans. We can only try and limit these by having systems and learning from the mistakes that happen.
2. As for people laughing at you – I think we'd all be surprised at how little others care about what we're doing. And I mean this in the nicest possible way. We often feel like people's eyes are burning into our soul (whether online or in real life!) and they aren't all that often. People are wrapped up in their own lives as much as we are all wrapped up in ours. I know you're special because you're reading these words and you've made the choice to grab the promotion of your brand by the bits, but everyone feels that they're special. I know when I publish this book, I will be excited but also feel sick. Because you know there's going to be a flipping typo and as an author you can't

have typos, can you? Cue the cycle. But the chances are that a lot of people won't spot the errors and the vast majority won't care. If anyone does and wants to be pleased that I made a mistake – well, they're not my tribe are they!? I really have zero interest in their opinion.

3. Last but not least – those 'laughing' people? Not only are they not your tribe, but you are lapping them because you are out there. You're doing your thing. You're living your life. And you're doing your best. So, and I mean this in the nicest possible way, screw them.

A while ago, I met a really inspirational lady called Victoria Knowles-Lacks. In addition to founding a forward thinking, fun and inclusive organisation to help ladies get out there and learn and enjoy clay shooting, Victoria has also weathered a fair few storms in her time, all of which she talks about in her superb book, Make It Happen. Here, she shares a few words of wisdom:

'You know that if people feel the need to judge you or put you down it really isn't about you, it's about them?

'This was such a powerful realisation and really changed things for me. People who act in a negative way towards you are actually just projecting their insecurities and beliefs on to you. So, for instance if someone does pick out your typos, tries to discredit you or just plain old wants to have a go, it's usually because they're fearful, and it's an insight into how they feel about themselves. You can't change these people, it needs to come from them. You can only change you, so always stay focussed on you.

'A real game changer for me when it came to making big progress was to embrace being imperfectly perfect. When I accepted that I wasn't brilliant at everything and all that I could do was my best, I felt like I became invincible. I let go of so much which really was rocket fuel for my business. Knowing we can't control everything is so powerful too. Similarly, you can't control the curveballs that undoubtedly will happen in your business, but you can control how you react and that's enough. React with good intentions and just let the rest go.

'Let go of other people's opinions, let go of being perfect and let go of what you can't control.'

Get comfortable with boasting

This is going to be a hard pill to swallow, but you're going to have to be comfortable with what you think of as boasting. Don't close the book, stay with me.

I'm British and I hate boasting. But I've drilled down into this a little and I've worked out why I hate it.

I can't tolerate boasting in others. By boasting, I mean people blowing their own trumpet when they don't have the clout, evidence or achievements to do it.

When someone has genuinely achieved something great and they dare to share it – what do you think? I don't think 'oh no, they're off again', if it's genuinely something that's worth talking about, I'm excited for them. When friends and people in my tribe ace something, I'm so pleased for them. I don't see it as boasting.

It might be worth having a little think on it. If you find the behaviour repulsive in others (and therefore don't want to see it in yourself), think why you find it so repulsive. Is it the language they use? The way they talk about what they've achieved? That their achievement isn't really an achievement in your eyes? What is it? Because I would bet money that you don't feel irritated because they did something good, that they should be proud of...and they shared it? It might even be that you're a little jealous of their success? This is all fine in my eyes, but if you find the real reason, it becomes much easier to process. If you process what it is that you don't like, you can make sure you don't do the same.

This isn't to say that you shouldn't tell people what you've done, but things can be tweaked so that it still promotes the same point but attacks it from a very different direction.

Over the years, I've been lucky enough to have a lot of good things happen for the clients that I work with. Big magazine features being one of them. When I was working in PR as my main 'gig', promoting what I'd managed to secure for a client was, and is, (let's be honest) a very good way to actually promote myself. Rather than me talking about how I would help to increase their exposure and get them in magazines, I had the evidence that I didn't just talk a good game. I could deliver the goods. I had it all there. But saying 'look at me, I'm God's gift to the world of PR – LOOK AT ME' made me feel sick to my stomach and I would never ever do it. It's not me. If you can and want to do this, own it, but in my experience, a lot of people feel uncomfortable about promoting themselves like this.

What I really wanted to do was promote my client. The fact I'd worked my backside off to get that feature was for them. One way I would do this was by promoting my client's feature [1] acknowledging how well they'd done and how proud I was of them and delighted that they'd been recognised. Because that was true. I was also (and am still) grateful to the magazine and enjoyed thanking them in public for what they'd done, because I appreciated it. And so did my clients. This felt easy and correct to me. I wanted to promote them and as a side benefit I was showing what I could do. Rather than it being all about me. Because as someone who hates that, it was too much. I also think that in the role as a PR, the client should always be the focus. You're not there to take the spotlight or the glory because you're being paid to get that for them.

How does that feel to you? While I appreciate this is just one example, think about it for a minute. If shouting from rooftops makes you want to vomit, you have to think of a different way to do it. You just have to.

If you're a service provider, shift the focus onto clients. If you make products, share a story behind the design. Or the suppliers of the elements. We'll look at lots of different ideas when we get into the different sections but trust me when I say that there will be a way and you just need to find it.

Imposter syndrome is a thing

Have you heard of this before? It's a really common thing, that it seems most people suffer with from time to time. It's that niggling feeling that you're about to be uncovered as a fraud. Yes, you. The professional who is expecting others to pay for what you do or make. You're about to be revealed as a fraud.

But the thing is, you're not a fraud if you tell the truth, are you? If you say you're a surgeon and you're not – then yes, we do have a problem (and quite a big one to be fair), but if you say you make and design scarves and you make and design scarves, you're good. You might not have a degree in design, or studied art at a swanky art school in Paris, or have qualifications in manufacture, or insert anything else you could possibly have in order to do the job, which you didn't say you did, did you?

I know so many people who have this. And if you do, you're not alone. In fact, I went to Google and asked to see famous people with imposter syndrome. Emma Watson – you know, HERMIONE GRANGER, Sheryl Sandberg – you know, THE CHIEF OPERATING OFFICER OF FACEBOOK, Maya Angelou, Amy Schumer, Tom Hanks, MICHELLE OBAMA. And there are loads more. When you go down this particular rabbit hole on Google, prepare to have your mind absolutely blown by the incredible people who have and continue to achieve amazing things, who think they're about to be 'revealed' as a fraud. Because when you think of Michelle Obama – what do you think? I think of a powerful, incredible, strong woman who's eloquent, intelligent and a real force for good. Fraud is not a word I would have ever connected to her.

A little while ago I interviewed Chloe Brotheridge, a hypnotherapist, mentor and coach at www.calmer-you.com and the host of The Calmer You Podcast. She's the author of The Anxiety Solution and The Confidence Solution. We talked about all things connected to anxiety and confidence with a particular bias towards social media and business, and she mentioned Imposter Syndrome. In fact, it was she who told me about Michelle Obama and made me wonder who else did too. Chloe explains a bit more about it here.

> 'Imposter syndrome is most common amongst successful women. Even incredibly smart and talented women like Michelle Obama have admitted to experiencing imposter syndrome. Depending on which survey you ask, between 60-90% of women will experience it at some point or another. You're not alone. We often doubt ourselves when doing something new, outside of our comfort zone or after experiencing a set back. It's normal and not a sign that you aren't good enough. Imposter syndrome could actually be a good

thing, a sign that you're growing and expanding. It's not a sign that you're not good enough.

'Imposter syndrome can be linked to perfectionism and a belief that no matter what we do, it won't be good enough.

'To overcome it, instead of putting your successes down to luck, think about what it was about you that made that success possible. Whether it's your work ethic, your great people skills or your creativity; give yourself credit.'

As you'll see from the above, mindset is really a key part of your success. I know when we flip our thinking, get our brains on side and feel as confident as we should, amazing things can happen.

Your top takeaways from this chapter:

- you've got to work on your mindset – it's a crucial part of your success or failure
- your first attempt at most stuff won't be great, but you have to do it to be great
- a lot of people, particularly women, feel that they're about to be uncovered as a fraud when they aren't.

Notes

1. Always ask permission from the publisher before you share any article anywhere.

3. In Print

You might think that traditional printed media is dead. And I don't want you to think that. Because even if you don't read magazines and newspapers, your target market might. For this reason you need to have printed media in your mind. I'm not saying you need to act on this thought, but you need to be aware of it.

Let's be honest though, readerships of magazines and newspapers are declining overall and have been for a few years. There are magazines who are bucking the trend, but they are definitely the exception. I was going to list some examples, but I decided against it because, first, these numbers move around all the time and, second, it doesn't feel fair to call magazines out when it's a general issue. Do you know what I mean? However, there's plenty of stories on pressgazette.co.uk (if you search ABC there's information on circulations) or the ABC website. ABC stands for Audit Bureau of Circulations and will show you the circulations of any publication registered with them (not all are). However, you can find out more about ABC at abc.org.uk.

But what's interesting is that in most cases (and in the niche I do most of my work in at least), advertising rates haven't gone down. If you were to place a paid for ad it might cost you more now than when the magazine had a much greater readership. On paper – or for the advertiser at least – this doesn't make a whole lot of sense. Especially when you consider that advertising online has the cost directly linked to the reach, number of clicks, or whatever metric you choose. But magazines are different. Because unlike an online system where you do the majority or all of the work and the process is automated, magazines still require manpower. They still require writers, photographers, designers, etc. They still require printing and if the readership has gone down, they are selling less magazines which means that their income is down from that side of things. Printing magazines costs a lot of money so while you might think 'well, they'll get less money but they're printing less', the sums aren't quite so easy as there's still design, production, editing and other costs to consider.

Magazines don't have an easy time of it. If they cut costs on the standard of the articles, imagery, editing or design, for example, let alone the paper quality, the overall calibre of the publication goes down. And if someone is paying around the £5 mark for a magazine and they get something that's really pretty rubbish, they might not buy it again. If the magazine cuts corners at any stage, the publication could suffer, the readership could take a hit and that makes it even harder to get those key advertisers.

But it's not all bad. The smart magazines and newspapers have also built incredible websites and have very active and engaged social media platforms that help to bridge the gap between the online and offline experience. Yes, the circulation of the magazine may have reduced, but their website, social media and whatever else has 'made up for it'. Or at least they've found ways to reach the volume of people that they need to in whatever format to 'secure' the publication as a whole, while still delivering to people who want to advertise.

Horse & Hound is a popular magazine within my niche and is seen as the leading light in equestrian circles; it's not called The Equestrian Bible for nothing. But with the rise in websites and social media it, like so many magazines, has seen a drop in readership. However, if there's one story about how even the most traditional publication can work with digital and social, this is it. In addition to printed features, Horse & Hound has a website editor and digital team that create content just for its online platforms. They even have paid options that provide exclusive content online to magazine subscribers and those who pay for the extra subscription online if they don't subscribe to the printed magazine. I should know, I write for the website periodically.

'Horse & Hound is fortunate to have a trusted, authoritative voice and a 136-year-old reputation for bringing exclusive news and expert insight to riders and equestrian enthusiasts, and that has allowed the publication to pivot from being a print only heritage brand to having a hugely successful website.

'The newsstand has been a challenging place for all print media over the past 10 years, and print has obvious limitations – for example it's easy to be timely online and much harder when you go to press four days before your media hits the shelves. We took the view that we would better serve readers by breaking the news online as it happened, and moving the story forward in print. We have a very loyal subscriber base and continue to delight these readers with a product they can feel and enjoy without straining their eyes. The magazine is full of longer readers, exclusive comments, in-depth reports and nostalgia, which readers can enjoy at their leisure. In contrast our website, in addition to providing breaking news anywhere on any device, provides a strong community with our highly engaged forum, gives readers the answers to all the questions they're looking for in search, entertains our strong social media following with humorous listicles and stories they can relate to – and which often pull at the heart strings. And of course the website became the place to buy and sell horses, with its immediacy and modern search functionality.

'Our editorial team work across our platforms, being as

skilled in SEO and video presenting as they are in constructing a print news story or long-form magazine interview. Our platforms do different things for different enthusiasts in different ways, and we continue to grow – be it with paid for digital content, awards, podcasts, events, or other brand extensions. Our team have the passion and expertise to deliver journalism the horse world wants, we just keep adapting to how people want to receive those stories.'

Sarah Jenkins, Horse & Hound Editor-in-Chief

I said it was important to think about where your people are. There are some niches and age brackets that are still all about printed media. How do you know if this applies to you and your customers? Ask them... simple as that.

You can do this through clever polls and questionnaires or just use an online resource like Survey Monkey and send it to people. When you do this, try not to show a bias – just ask straight questions. You don't want to overwhelm people with a three million question survey, but you do want to learn from the process.

If you're not sure if your target market buys magazines simply ask questions like 'when did you last buy a magazine or newspaper?', 'how often do you buy magazines or newspapers?', 'which magazines do you buy?'. Think about what you want to learn from asking these questions and then just ask.

If you don't fancy a questionnaire, you can run polls on social media, or just straight up ask your customers the question. Or you can do a mixture of all of the above.

Magazines and newsletters will also have a lot of information relating to their readership in their media packs. You'll often find out things such as age range, income, hobbies, all sorts. Media packs contain this to attract the right advertisers to them, and to show you a glimpse of who your advert could be shown to. Just contact the magazines you're interested in working with and ask for this.

Using your fans and followers and customer feedback from this can help you identify whether or not you should invest any or some time in the world of print. For the rest of this section, I'm going to assume the answer is yes...

Get your research on

If you followed the steps above, you could well have a list of magazines that your target market has said they read. Some of these might be red herrings. If you sell a product, let's say, clothing for children, and one of your customers is also a very keen motorbike enthusiast, that's your red herring. But equally if a lot of your target market mentions a specific magazine, even if it feels a bit left field to you, it might be worth exploring.

When you have a few magazines that you think tick the boxes, buy them and look at them. And I mean really look at them. What do you see?

What kind of features do they run? What features are free 'editorial' style features – like new products, buyers' guides, tried and tested, etc? Which have adverts, advertorials or advertising features in them? What features could your product or service sit in? Do they have any interview style pieces that you could potentially get involved with? Who is responsible for that feature (there's often a writer's name on the feature). If you can't see it, go to the front of the magazine and you'll likely find a contacts list – look at the job titles and see who would probably be in charge of the sections you could fit in, and if you have no idea, just call the main phone number or email the contact email or editorial assistant and ask. They don't bite. And if you're polite and courteous you'll go a long way.

You don't have to stress yourself out when you call – just a simple 'Hi there, I hope you can help me, I was wondering who edits this part of your magazine/newspaper and if I might be able to have his/her details as I'd love to speak to her/him about how I might be able to get involved' is all you need to start. Thank anyone who's been kind enough to help you for their time and for giving you the information you need. These contacts could help you to supercharge your business and allow it to help you achieve your goals. It sounds over dramatic, doesn't it? But think of what a big glossy feature in a magazine that's perfect for your target market could do for your business. It might not be transformative but it's a big step.

Build your contacts

When you're hooked up to the right people, again, be respectful. Generally, people who work in traditional media are busy as busy can be. They have more deadlines than you can shake a stick at, there's probably less people around than you think to do everything, and you want to interrupt their day and their to do list so they can help you.

I'm not saying this to put you off. I'm just outlining the facts, so when you make your approach you can keep this firmly in mind and be polite but succinct with what you say. Depending on the feature you'd like to be in, you might want to ask for a features list or forward feature list that might highlight a list of themes, products they're testing or items they want to feature in which issue. Brilliant. If that's the case then you could add a couple of lines about what you do too, but not your whole history about how you first developed a love of whatever before you could walk. Make your request clear and obvious early on. This means that if your editor is, indeed, super busy, there's a much better chance that they'll see what you want. Something like this:

> 'Hi A,
>
> B gave me your details as I run a business called C, specialising in D. I would really appreciate it if you would be able to send me a forward features list so I can see what you have coming up and what I might be able to get involved with if you have space.'

Most features lists have deadlines and some also show things like word count and even exactly what the editor wants to receive. For things like tried and tested features this might be the size of the product and the address to send along with RRP, colours, 50 words of text, contacts, high res image, etc. This will be different from publication to publication. You may need to ask, but that's fine too. Get the list, see if anything fits, then ask.

Martha Keith from marthabrook.com has some interesting thoughts on super sleuthing when it comes to magazines and the ability to make valuable connections by doing the work.

> 'At Martha Brook, we've never used a PR agency but have been lucky enough to have been widely featured in the press – from Forbes to the Independent to Glamour, to name a few – purely through some super sleuthing! Although many digital outlet magazines have partnerships with the bigger brands, they are always interested in featuring smaller independent businesses, especially if the product is newsworthy, topical or exciting. Journalists do not mind you contacting them

and actually love to hear from the business founder themselves.

'Firstly think about which publications you'd like to be featured in, do some research on the journalists writing the features and hunt down their email address online, then drop them a short email with the product, website link, RRP and why it is of interest. Always have high res images ready – these are key – you will need these if they want to feature you. It does take some time to put the work in, but I would highly recommend giving it a go. I am a great believer that if you don't ask, you don't get!'

Get on a press list

Now you have your contact, you have a further opportunity for two things. First, to be added to their press list. This is a good one. Some magazines have a list of contacts at companies, PR agencies and more that they email when they need something for a feature. Maybe it's a full on shoot they're planning and they need everything. Or maybe they have been let down by someone and they need something pronto. Ask if you can be added.

Second, ask if you can add them to your list of contacts. Don't have a press list? You do now. Well, if they say yes, you do. Your press list can become a massively valuable string to your bow and will allow you to send news and new information, often in the format of a press release, to said person. This is valuable. Trust me.

If you're building your press list from the ground up (as you should do), you will start with one contact. This will be a contact that has given you permission to be added to your list, who you have emailed or chatted to and your product or service is relevant for their publication or website. Keep adding one name at a time as you ask and get permission to do so. It's that simple.

Relationships

It's not all about the list though. It's the people on that list and, more to the point, the relationships you nurture with people that can help you.

There's a theme in this book and that's the power of one. And I believe this wholeheartedly. It is better to have one editor who gets and loves what you do, that you chat to and send information and products to, than it is to have a faceless list of, I don't know, a thousand people who couldn't care less. They're extreme numbers but true. You're so much more likely to get your press releases and emails read by people who get you and are interested, than those who aren't.

But isn't this limiting you?

If you stick at one person it might not be the strongest strategy, granted, but the idea is that you look to form these connections one at a time.

Not only can you gain from this connection but if done properly, the editor should too. If you prioritise their needs, know how they like to work and how they like to receive the information; you're making their life easier. I've had many an email or phone call from an editor asking me for something when they've been let down by other companies...and that means that I, or my clients, gain the advantage because the editor knows me and knows I will do anything I can to help them.

Through relationships I've bagged regular columns in relevant magazines for clients, columns for myself, big articles, small articles, regular mentions, news snippets; you name it. As my relationships with editors and magazines have grown, I've been able to understand their needs more, their readership and everything else. And this means that in addition to all the above when I have a new product and a new idea for a feature, my pitch will be better. If the pitch is better and more relevant to their audience, then I'm more likely to get that approved. See what I mean?

Another great thing about this is it won't cost you a fortune and you don't need anyone else to help you do it. If you work along the idea that one person has the ability to make a big difference, then you only need to focus on one person at a time – how good is that? Just one person to contact and connect with. Then go for another. And another. Go one at a time and you will get there.

Submit

With all of the above in place, you will still need to deliver the goods. As mentioned above, sometimes the features list will explain exactly what is needed and sometimes it won't. If you're in any doubt about it, just ask.

Generally, short and to the point wins when it comes to any feature that's not just about you – like a tried and tested or product round up – but there's no harm in asking.

In addition to the information (product details, price, etc) you're submitting, you also need to be really aware of the deadline and the images, if any, that you need to submit.

Get the images right

When you send images to a printed publication, you need to be aware that these aren't the same as images on your website. Generally, website images are much smaller and low resolution. This means that they load quickly (which is a big deal in today's impatient world!), but it also means that when printed on paper the images can be pixelated (blocky and a bit rubbish). You'll also notice that most file sizes for web images are really small.

For print, images need to be high resolution (usually 300dpi). Some magazines also specify a size for images, too. These images would take much longer to load on a website, but when printed, show crisp, clear edges and detail, which is exactly what you want.

Images for print will vary in size and it pays to be aware of this, as breaking someone's inbox will not win you any fans. This is much rarer nowadays (you're more likely to be the straw that broke the camel's back in terms of capacity vs actually breaking it!) but still, just don't. If you need to add a number of images to your email and the size is adding up, you can use services like Dropbox, WeTransfer or similar to send your files.

With Dropbox, you'd put the relevant images into a folder then share the link to that folder in an email for the recipient to download when they like. With services like WeTransfer, the recipient needs to click a link and then download a file to their desktop. Both work well in their own way. I personally prefer Dropbox because the images are there until the person chooses to delete/move them whereas there's a time limit on WeTransfer. It's horses for courses. There are plenty of other options available that do the same thing. I just mentioned these two as I have the most experience with them.

What type of images do you need for magazines?

Before we leave images for print altogether, it might be a good idea to have a chat about the kind of images you might need for magazines.

Have a look at the magazines you've shortlisted as relevant to you, what kind of images do they use? Are they using images where it's the product on its own with a white background (also known as a studio shot or packshot) or are they using a staged or posed image with a person (if clothing), in a relevant setting, or as a flatlay, for example, with lots of different things going on?

In my experience, if you had to have just one type, packshot or studio is likely to serve you better with magazines because it allows them to design the page in their style with less effort. If they want to feature 10 different products on a page and each has a different lifestyle angle with a different editing technique, it's not going to look all that cohesive. With a studio shot that's then cut out, the options are endless.

Getting these images might feel like a big stress, but it doesn't have to be. If you have the budget you can send products away for packshot photography (or find a local photographer with the relevant kit or studio) or arrange a shoot to get some great lifestyle images that you can send to magazines and use for other things too.

A quick note on press releases

I've mentioned press releases a few times above and although

I'm not going to go into how to write a press release here, I want to tell you why you should take the time to do it.

Some people will tell you that press releases are outdated. But I want to say that in my experience they aren't, if you use them properly. Yes, the first purpose of the press release is indeed to inform the press (and your press list) about what's going on, what's new or newsworthy. But it doesn't have to end there. You can repurpose your beautifully written piece of work for further good. I like this method too because it means that even if the magazine doesn't use your press release, your time hasn't been wasted.

One really simple way to repurpose your press release is to make it into a blog. One adjustment I would make here is shifting it from third person to first person and remove the quote if your press release has one. Because, especially if you're a smaller business and your tone is more conversational, referring to yourself in the third person can be a bit jarring and seem a bit distant.

That said, some people have 'press release' areas on their website that are just that – areas where they publish their press releases and, in that case, keep it as it is and also add links that will allow people to download the relevant images to go with it. In your blogs you'd be more likely to embed the images to read like an article on a website.

Guarantees and usage

The 'problem' with 'free' editorial is that there are no guarantees... but that's the name of the game. If you pay to be included, whether you've paid for an advert or advertorial to secure further inclusion that way, that's a different animal. With things like buyers' guides, press releases, news and product rounds ups, it's at the editor's discretion. If you don't get picked, don't take it to heart – OK? There will be lots of people trying to get in each feature. Even if you do everything right you won't get in every feature all the time – it's just the name of the game, but it makes it all the sweeter when you do.

And when you do get published?

Celebrate. There's something about seeing yourself or your product/service in print that just feels very special. It's funny that something printed can feel more valuable than something online, isn't it?

Obviously, you'll want to share this achievement on places like your social media, but ALWAYS ask permission from the publisher, even if you're planning to take a flatlay image of the article for your social. You still need to ask permission. You could be fined if you don't.

4. Social Media

I'm not going to lie to you and say I'm ambivalent about social media – I'm not – I love it. For my business, social media has allowed me to connect with and work with businesses all over the globe. My first TEDx talk was about this subject and showed how it connected me to a lovely lady based in New Zealand and then how social media allowed her to work with a lady in Norway. I struggled to pronounce the name of her hometown (Purakaunui – which is pronounced poo-raa-car-noo-ey... seriously, imagine trying to pronounce that when you're pretty stressed about the whole situation!), but it was all good fun and kind of worked out – you can see that TEDx talk if you head over to YouTube and search 'Rhea Freeman TEDx', if you fancy a little trip around the world. It's allowed me to reach out to people I wouldn't have been able to get access to pre social media. It's allowed me to get to know people a whole lot better and engage with them – giving them the chance to get to know me before they decide to work with me. And it's helped me find lots of stuff that I 'needed' but didn't know existed!

Not everyone loves social media. It's crazy to me to think that as I write this now, my husband doesn't even have a Facebook account. Or an Instagram account. And my father in law once referred to Facebook as 'you know, the book face'. The secret is, you don't have to love social media. You don't even have to like it. But for your business, you need to see its value and you need to tap into that.

A brief history of social media

You might not be able to remember a world without social media but it did, in fact, exist. According to Social Media Today,[1] the first social media site, called Six Degrees, started in 1997, but the one we all know about (that is still around today) is Facebook, which came onto the scene in 2004.

Facebook

As you may or may not know, Facebook was originally created as a platform for people in schools, colleges and universities to use to connect with each other... but not now.

Since its launch, not only has Facebook grown in size (it now has 2.9 billion monthly active users according to Facebook in Q1 2021,[2] but the range of services it offers and the functionality built in is simply astounding. No longer a place for just text and images, you can live stream, post videos, enjoy 'watch parties'... the list is almost endless and I'm sure will continue to grow.

Instagram

The next most popular social media platform at the time of writing is Instagram, which is also part of the Facebook group of platforms.

Over one billion people use Instagram each month.[3] ONE BILLION. Just to put the scale of this (and, of course, Facebook's numbers) into perspective, according to United Nations, there are around 7.8 billion people on the planet (February 2021) so it's a fairly impressive percentage, isn't it?

Instagram burst into our lives in 2010 and although I'm not going to explain all the features here, it's safe to say that since the first image was shared, it's come on a bit. With various different features like Stories, Direct Messages, Reels, video, hashtags and so much more introduced at various stages, Instagram is now more than just a place to share your favourite holiday snaps. Although it is still pretty good for that too!

In 2012, Instagram was sold to Facebook for $1 billion.[4] Which I think we can all agree is not too bad for a few years' work(!). Of course, since that sale, Instagram has come on leaps and bounds and has become a really big part of the social media landscape as the numbers alone show.

YouTube

If video is your media of choice (for creation or consumption) then YouTube will likely be somewhere you'll hang out.

Owned by Google, YouTube is more than just a video sharing site; it's a search engine too. If you're anything like me, you spend a lot of your life searching 'how do I...', which is often followed by all manner of random things (like, how to buff a scratch out of the car using toothpaste, how to make a good omelette, and how to dismantle a vacuum cleaner – these are actual searches I have done!). But in addition to being somewhere you can go to learn how to do all the domestic things you need to in life, YouTube is a whole lot more.

Because I like the stats (and find YouTube's mind blowing!), here are a few. If you go to YouTube's own press centre, you'll find an array of incredible numbers. Over one billion users and one billion hours of YouTube watched daily speak to me as stats. Don't you think?

It's also worth noting that if you host your video on YouTube, you can then share that link on social if you fancy, but you can also embed said link into your website. This means that if people want to learn more about your products and services, they can watch at no extra stress or cost to you!

Pinterest

If you've found yourself down a Pinterest 'pinning' (Pinterest's way of organising and curating content) rabbit hole at any time, it's fair to say that you're not alone... there's a lot going on there.

Pinterest has over 430 million monthly active users.[5] It's a real source of inspiration for so many things. But don't think it's all about interiors and children's birthday cakes. It isn't.

If Pinterest is a source of inspiration, which it is, this inspiration can move beyond the home and spread into the world of fashion, cookery, business... you name it. I also think that Pinterest has some really nice features that integrate well into other areas, like the Pin button you can add to images on your website to allow others to pin your content, and the Pin 'add on' you can add to your internet browser that allows you as a consumer to pin things you like, want to remember, and want take inspiration from.

Twitter

I feel a bit sorry for Twitter in many ways. So many people are negative about it and say it's ailing... that is until Facebook and/ or Instagram break... and you know where social media users flock? Yep – you guessed it – Twitter.

Twitter started life in 2006 and and there are said to be over 390 million monthly active users of the platform.[6] Twitter has always had a pretty small character count, which was just 140 character until late 2017 when the number was doubled to 280. Hashtags continue to be popular on Twitter, and although you can share images, videos and even live content, I tend to see Twitter as more of a place for conversations – and fast paced ones at that.

There are some industries that seem to particularly enjoy the use of Twitter – journalism is one. In fact, have a search of #journorequest and when you make your way beyond the sea of bloggers using the hashtag incorrectly (in my opinion), you could well find a lovely little opportunity or two to promote whatever you're doing.

Snapchat

Snapchat was founded in 2011 and in in Q1 2022 reported 332 million daily active users.[7]

Snapchat is often associated with the younger generation and was different to other platforms when it launched because the content shared wasn't permanent. You could send a 'snap' to someone and it wouldn't be around for long, and you could also add filters too.

Like all the other platforms, Snapchat has grown and developed and generated different functionality to allow it to stand out from the crowd for its own unique selling points, which I do like. I have to admit that it's not a platform I spend a whole lot of time on... but we'll talk about that later!

TikTok

TikTok is a baby in the world of social media, but wow, it's certainly made a big impact in just a few years.

TikTok is well known for its short videos, often set to music, that allow people to express themselves. From challenges that unite people around common and important themes to ones designed to make people smile, educational content (I follow an amazing psychologist and doctor who share lots of information in short videos), to simply sharing experiences. TikTok is fun and engaging. And it's not just me who thinks so, in fact, it's reported to have 755 million monthly active users.[8]

Recently, TikTok has started to add additional features that put it in direct competition with other platforms. Stories are one and TikTok Shop is another. It's definitely a platform to keep a very close eye on and get involved with if it is right for you.

LinkedIn

The last one I'm going to touch on here is LinkedIn, because if you're reading this and you're a business to business (often called B2B) brand, it might be a place to consider hanging out.

LinkedIn was founded in 2003 and now has 830 million members.[9] The thing about LinkedIn, though, is that it's not about the numbers, it's the quality of the connections you can make there. And going back to the power of one theme, these connections could be incredibly valuable due to the platform.

As the only 'pure' business to business platform, it's a great place for networking and 'meeting' people in the business world. I've genuinely found work through LinkedIn, was invited to speak at an event, and have made some really good connections that have helped me and my business. It seems to move at a much slower pace to some of the other platforms, but it's there for a different purpose too – I see LinkedIn a bit like a networking event that you don't need to brush your hair to go to.

Where do you start?

If you've looked at all the information above and started to sweat, please don't. While the list above can seem overwhelming, please PLEASE don't think you need to be on all these platforms, all the time, because you don't, OK?

With a bit of research you'll find where your target market hang out and, therefore, where you might want to be. If you look at the demographics of people who use the platforms (Google will help you out here, as will the press areas of the different platforms) you'll be able to get an idea of where your customers are. If you're pitching at ladies who are 50 plus, for example, the chances are Snapchat might not be somewhere to focus a whole lot of time and energy. Of course, there will be some 50 year old ladies on Snapchat but the likelihood is that there might not be enough (and there will be other platforms where the numbers are greater), to make it worth the time and energy you're going to need to spend on the platform to get established.

You will need to do this, because the best way to work these platforms out is to use them. Set up your own accounts and just explore how it all works. Because if you don't really understand the features, functions and what it can do, you're unlikely to get the best out of the platform and you really do want to do that.

Start with one

It sounds scary, but if you're not using any social media at all at the moment, just start with one. The one you think is most likely to be where your target customers are hanging out and work hard there. When you feel like you've got a fairly good handle on what's going on and how it all works, think about adding another platform. Think of it like plate spinning – you have to get the first one up and twirling before you get a second one going.

If you do try and use them all at once, you could well leave yourself feeling a bit confused, overwhelmed and despondent with social media – and I don't want you to do that because it is incredible when used properly. Get yourself established on one, then add another.

Type of content on social media

Now we move into the fun stuff. As I don't know which platforms you've picked, the headings below are broad but I'm trusting you to work out exactly what will work best on the platforms that you have picked. I don't want you to think you're going to nail it to start with, because you won't. You'll spend ages working on, I don't know, a video, and the text will get cut in half when you post. Or you'll manage to do something amazing that you couldn't repeat if you were paid a lot of money to do it again, but you've managed it. We've all done it!

Make your images work hard

Let's just start at the top – images. Images are such a huge part of social media and one where, to be honest, you can make some huge wins. Even if you're not a photographer and plan to use your phone for every single image on your social media, there's no excuse not to have great images that you share and post.

As you scroll through your social media feeds, start to notice the images and I reckon you'll be amazed at the range. You'll see some that have every filter applied, some that are harshly edited and smooth out every laughter line, some that have been edited to look more dreamy or vibrant, or pick up on the latest editing techniques. Then you'll find some that are completely unedited and look good, and others that are too dark, too light, blurry – you'll see the whole spectrum. But it's important to see this. What images make you stop scrolling? Are they the crisp, clear ones or the ones like an old school 'magic eye' picture that you move in and out to see if you can work out what the heck is going on before working out whether or not you should care? I'm the former. I don't have the time for optical illusions.

You want your images to do so much. They say a picture paints a thousand words, but on social media, a picture can also stop someone's busy finger from scrolling on beyond your content and encourage them to read on. The right images have the power to let people into your world, to show a bit of your brand and the look/feel/vibe on a deeper level, to show a product in an enticing way, to show love and connection – seriously – it's endless. And now think of what a bad image can show? What do you think when you see a poor quality image on your social media feed?

Before you think 'hang on, she said this marketing stuff didn't have to cost a fortune and now I need a clever camera, editing software and professional shoots all the time' chill out. You don't. Your phone and an eye for detail along with some top tips is all you actually need. If you want to and have funds for a professional shoot, then please do seriously consider it as you can get massive value from pro shots in all sorts of ways. But because this book is all about how to do it on a shoestring, that is our focus.

Sophie Callahan is a specialist equine photographer who also undertakes commercial photography for businesses with a country or equine connection. In addition to this, she's also a blogger, vlogger and has amassed an impressive number of followers across her own social media platforms. If she doesn't know the value of good quality imagery, no one does. And better still, she's got tips to share to improve your photography too.

1. For the best photographs, you need to begin with the best light. In almost all cases, this will be using natural light, but in an area of 'open shade'. If you are indoors, look for a spot by the window that isn't in direct sunlight and if you are outdoors, the shade of a building or tree is perfect.

2. Always check your composition. Make sure you have a nice clear margin around your subject, make sure you haven't cropped any of the product out, unintentionally and ensure that your background doesn't include anything undesirable, like a rubbish bin, distracting signs or even horse poo! A clean background and good composition will draw the viewers eye to your subject.

3. It sounds obvious, but always make sure your subject is actually *in focus!* You would be amazed

how many photos I've seen that are totally out of focus. If you're using a camera phone, you can tap the subject on the screen and it will bring it into focus for you.

4. Invest in learning how to edit. If you'd like to take beautiful photos for your business, yourself, I'd highly recommend looking into learning how to edit an image. You don't need to know anything super fancy, but just adjusting exposure, white balance, contrast and colour can make a huge difference. Editing (whether using purchased, ready made presets or doing it manually) can also help make all of your brand images appear uniform and cohesive. I'd highly recommend Adobe Lightroom for both desktop and mobile editing.

Create graphics easily

I love a graphic – and they are SO easy to create. You can create graphics for any time you want to share words in a visual format. Think quotes, testimonials, top tips, etc.

You might think that you need to have graphic design experience and/or expensive software to make your own graphics but you really don't. I use and adore Canva (https://www.canva.com), which is free, online and super easy to use, it makes creating graphics a breeze. It even has templates that you can customise and make your own. (I should say here that although I use Canva, I am aware of other pieces of software that others love, so don't think there's only Canva in the whole world, but it's a good place to start!)

When you're creating graphics, keep in mind you can use images, solid colours or patterns for the background and you can be as creative with the fonts as you like. I know there is a real knack to graphic design (and it's not something I have ever trained in so I'm telling you this from experience and not a lot else) but be careful with the fonts you use and how many of them you employ. Sometimes less is more.

There are SO many fonts out there, but I think the key with any graphic is that the font is easy to read. Again, think of the finger stopping power of something profound that people can read quickly vs. an elaborate script font that's just SO hard to decipher. Be aware of your colour choices against the background (again, think easy to read) and be aware of the number of different fonts you use per image. There's lots of information online about this (in fact, Canva does have online learning resources around this) and it's worth spending some time studying your social media feeds and thinking hard about what works for you and what doesn't. As per... well... everything in life, what people 'like' is subjective and based on their views and nothing else... so don't try and make everyone happy because you won't do it. But creating something that's hard to read is not likely to win you too many fans.

Another thing to keep in mind when you create a graphic is how 'on brand' it is. Most brands have a colour palette that's connected to them. For my brand, I have burgundy as the main colour and then use white, green, grey and sometimes pink. I have the hex colours for them all, and this means that when I use different software and enter the hex code (this starts with a # and is then a combination of specific letters and numbers), I know it's going to be the right burgundy/green/grey. Equally with fonts I have a few that are on brand for me and appear in things like the headings on my website. Having the same colours and fonts is a really easy way of creating a more cohesive, on brand and professional look without a whole heap of effort. It's really hard to match colours up by eye.

As for what to put on graphics – here are a few ideas for you.

1. Quotes – inspirational and motivational ones are great.
    Ones that you've come up with that tick the boxes are
    even better. Quotes tend to perform really well on social
    media.
2. Testimonials – instead of you blowing your own trumpet,
    let someone else do it with a testimonial.
3. Podcast extracts – each week I produce a podcast (The
    Small & Supercharged™ Podcast to be precise!) and each
    week I pull at least one quote from it that I post on social
    media a few days after it's been released. It's a great way to
    promote 'older' content without delivering the same
    message. It might also appeal to someone who wasn't
    attracted by the image that I posted but who the quote
    really resonates with.
4. Blog extracts – much like podcast extracts, adding a quote
    from a blog to a graphic can be really useful as sometimes
    the images don't cut the mustard for a long piece of
    written content, but a juicy quote might do.
5. Hashtag days/tips – if you want to get involved with
    hashtag days on social media, like #motivationmonday for
    example, you could create graphics around these. It's also
    a nice way to display a tip, such as on #tiptuesday.

This is not an exhaustive list but it's a start!

One last note about graphics; not all platforms are optimised
for the same sized graphic or image. If you look up current sizes
for whatever platform you want, you should find these quite
easily. Canva gives you the option to choose whether you want
your social media image for Facebook, Pinterest, whatever.
There's also another option I tend to pick inside Canva which
is just a square and that works pretty well on everything. It
might not be perfect for every platform BUT it will work on
every platform and that's important. It depends on how many

platforms you want to use your graphic on. If you're using it on only one, have a look at the best size for that platform as it might just give you a little bit more space when people scroll (like a portrait image vs. a landscape image on your Instagram feed, for example). It's just a little consideration that might give you an edge.

Connect with captions

Images and graphics are great and they're going to stop people scrolling, but the caption is your chance to connect, so put the work in here.

Depending on the platform, your caption might be long or short. By which I mean some platforms (like Twitter) will only let you have a maximum of 280 characters in a tweet, so don't bother writing an A4 page for that one, it just won't be seen unless you ask people to click away.

There's a bit of an art to writing a good caption; these are the best tips I have.

1. For most people, writing your caption like you talk is likely to work the best (unless you're a professional organisation and it's not appropriate for example).
2. Connect through the caption. Don't write as if it's a for sale ad – you're not advertising in the conventional sense through your social media, so don't make your captions do this. For example:

This high quality sterling silver ring was crafted by silversmiths in Kent and incorporates garnet gemstones from Peru. It's available in sizes A-M and has a RRP of £90.

We just love this ring! It's made in the UK by the most amazing silversmith in the South East of England and has the prettiest deep red gemstone at the front – do you know what it's called? We'll give you a clue – the name of the stone is connected to pomegranates!

While version one is more like a sales ad, which do you think is likely to get the most engagement? I'll take the second one any day of the week because, to me, I would be much more likely to engage with that and also, I don't feel like I'm being sold to. But have I learned about the product? Oh yes. Have I answered the question? Yes. So even if I'm not after a garnet ring at the moment, I'm more likely to remember the pomegranate comment than the other. See what I mean?

1. Include a call to action. This is such a good one. Ask for people's opinion, the answer to a question, a recommendation to encourage engagement – and good engagement at that. Starting a dialogue with someone is a great way to make these real connections that I talk about on my social media until the cows come home. If

the social media platforms 'see' that your content is engaging, it's likely to be seen by more people and so you're fuelling your own success. But please, PLEASE, if someone makes the effort to engage with your comment, comment back. Or at the very least acknowledge them. We're not on social media to sell, we're there to build relationships and connections to help support our businesses and brands. Asking someone a question, them answering, and then you ignoring them is like you asking someone a question at a party, them answering, and then you walking away. Don't do it!

2. Don't waffle, but don't fear a longer caption either. If you have something to say, then go for it, but don't just add words in for the sake of it.

3. Break it up. Think of the difference between a broken up block of text vs a solid block. One feels inviting, one feels like you might need a cuppa to get through it.

4. Do your best to avoid spelling mistakes. You'll make some but a once over will (hopefully) help you reduce how many you have.

5. Links. Some platforms allow you to include links inside the caption and others don't. You might not want to include links every time but it might be a good thing to experiment with to see if you get the clicks or not.

6. Hashtags. On Instagram in particular, there's an ongoing discussion about where to put the hashtags – in the first comment or in the caption. If you opt for caption (I do) then think about separating it with a few line breaks (so where you put a – then press return to form a new line) to make it appear less congested.

Tips and tricks

I could fill a whole book with tips and tricks when it comes to social media, and actually many people have. The reason that I didn't opt for a book all about social media was that I felt by the time I'd written it, new things would have come out and it would, therefore, not be as relevant as it could have been. When you look at these tips and tricks connected to social media, keep this in mind. The way that the algorithms work change and evolve so much. The features change and develop all the time, so the advice below is broad for these reasons.

Consistency is key

Consistency is such a big one, and not just for social media but for any marketing or promotional activity.

You need to have a surprisingly high number of touch points with someone before you make a sale. If you Google it, most people say around seven. But my gut feeling is that it's more than that now. There's SO much out there that I feel like I have information overload on a daily basis and with so many bits of stuff to process, I feel like I need more of them!

A touch point isn't just through a social media post, your points can be made up of different forms of contact, but the key is you really do need to make these points. And do you know how you're going to do that? By showing up. Again. And again. And again.

So many people give up too soon. They say the algorithm is not showing their content to their followers, that no one cares/is seeing/is engaging. So yes, the algorithm absolutely does limit the reach of posts, but that's not an excuse to have a tantrum and throw in the towel. What many people say and, I see in my own experience too, is that good posts that encourage and then get engagement early on will do better. By this I mean they kind of help themselves, so the more early engagement a post gets, the better it will do on a 'long' term basis on your social media. The inverted commas around long are because nothing is really that long term on social media and the amount of time differs for different platforms.

If you've got over that and taken on the initial limited reach as a challenge rather than a roadblock, we can address the other issue. That no one cares. The thing is, you don't know who's seeing your posts. You can see the numbers but you can't tell what influence that had on the person seeing it. Or who they were.

I've had numerous times when I've received an email or direct message from someone telling me how much they've enjoyed a podcast/post/video/whatever and how much they could relate to it or how it helped them. I really do get the warm fuzzies when this happens, but you know the weird thing? That some of these lovely people use a tone that is very chatty and friendly, like you would to a friend, but they have never contacted me before. Actually, I'm not even sure how much some of them have engaged with my content openly to that point. But they were watching. Because if they hadn't been, it wouldn't have helped them, and they definitely wouldn't have reached out.

Another thing on consistency before we move on (I'm nothing if not consistent on my quest to talk about consistency!) is that I like to think of my social media as my own media network. Like a TV show in some ways. Now, let's think about a TV show – a big one. I'm thinking Downton Abbey. I defy anyone who watched this programme not to find themselves invested in the characters. Willing Lady Mary to be a bit nicer to Matthew. SPOILER ALERT, shedding a tear (and promising to never forgive ITV) when they killed off Matthew on Christmas Day just after Lady Mary had given birth (I'm still not OK with this!). I could go on. But I was invested in these people. And I knew that each Sunday during the season, my screen would be graced with the latest witty one liners from the Dowager and a whole lot more. And I looked forward to it.

But now, imagine your favourite TV programme, that you're invested in. Now imagine you have no idea when it's going to be on next, or whether it will even come back at all. How invested would you be in it then?

Through our social media we want to attract our tribe, our cheerleaders, and people who root for us. But if they have no idea when we'll be there or if we'll even bother to appear again, why would they be so invested? We need to give people the chance to get on board with us. Some won't and that's fine but the ones who want to, help them out by turning up, please.

Be authentic

As I write this chapter there's a HUGE buzz around being authentic online. Which sounds completely bizarre if you're someone that doesn't know how to be any other way.

The thing is, if you're authentic online, and by which I mean you're yourself, the connections you make through your social media are going to be so much more valuable. Why? Because the people who get behind you are connecting with the real version of you. If you've created this incredible persona online but actually, in real life you couldn't be more different, I think you really have to question the value of that, don't you? Because if someone follows you or likes content you've created that isn't at all on brand then, really, who is that benefiting in the long run?

When I talk about authenticity I don't just mean words, I mean appearances too. There has, for a while, been a trend of being flawless in your imagery. This involves a range of different ideas including only posting professional images on your grid, not posting if there was so much as a hair out of place, only posting you were looking your best and then serious editing, air brushing and a few filters too, for good measure.

I know there are so many reasons why people use all the filters, and if that is you and it makes you feel more confident or achieves whatever you want it to, then you should absolutely embrace them. But please don't imply that that is real life. There are some really crazy things you can do to your image online, you can quite literally change the size of every bit of you, to make it look more 'perfect', but I'd urge you to dig deep before you go down this harsh route for the reasons above and so many more.

Use hashtags

I've mentioned hashtags previously but, particularly on Instagram and Twitter, hashtags can make content a lot more discoverable. You'll find trending hashtags (ones that are used a lot at the moment), hashtags relating to key events, TV programmes, you name it. Using relevant hashtags allows your content to be categorised by that hashtag so if people are searching for something via hashtag, your content will be in there.

Of course, using a hashtag doesn't guarantee your way to fame and fortune, but it does increase your chances of being discovered by people who don't already follow you but share similar passions. And it's literally the work of a moment to add a hashtag – but do always make sure that they are relevant, for everyone's sake.

Use it as a consumer

The best way to really understand social media is to use it. Get involved and use it like a consumer, not just a brand who's using it to broadcast. By finding out about the functions inside it, learning how they work and trying them out, you're going to be a whole lot better equipped to implement them. Reading about how things work is one thing, and it's a great place to start, but actually applying them is a different thing altogether.

Get engaged

When we use social media for our brand and the promotion of it, we want people to engage with us. They won't always buy what we have to offer, but a like, a share, a save, a comment, a direct message, can be hugely valuable and not just in an obvious way. Having someone take the time to comment on our posts can make us feel much better about whatever we've posted about, but it also gives us a great opportunity to connect with that user. Not necessarily in a way that will lead to a purchase.

If people engage with your content ENGAGE BACK. It's a conversation and I don't want you to be one of those people getting the weird looks, OK? Because if you add in a call to action, such as 'what do you think about this?' and someone responds, and you don't, you've basically blanked them.

When we use social media to build any kind of brand or business, we are looking to get to know people and form valuable connections. When someone essentially reaches out to you and tries this, you have a real opportunity there to make an important link. Maybe even a crucial link. So, take it. Please.

Jasmine Star is a bit of a hero of mine. Not only is her podcast (The Jasmine Star Show) my companion on many a dog walk, but her work as a brand strategist and photographer is incredible and aspirational. Jasmine is pretty passionate about engagement on social media – in fact, here are some tips from her about improving engagement on Instagram.

'There are no shortcuts when it comes to getting engagement.

So if you are willing to do the work and build genuine relationships with your followers, let's dive in to 3 steps you can take **every day** to triple your Instagram engagement.

1. Leave a thoughtful comment of at least four words on 10 follower's accounts – The lowest hanging fruit that will get the quickest results is to drive engagement with people who already follow you.

2. Post a poll in your stories, then respond via DM to everyone who voted – When you're communicating privately with your followers in their DMs, they know, like, and trust you.

3. Choose a hashtag and leave a comment of more than 4 words on 10 accounts – Once you find an appropriate hashtag, go to 10 accounts and leave a thoughtful comment on their most recent post. This may cause them to go to your account to follow and engage with you!'

You can read more about these three amazing tips on Jasmine's blog 'How to triple your Instagram engagement' at www.jasminestar.com.

Mix it up

Social media isn't all about the sale – the clue is in the name – it should be social. It's a free place to promote yourself as a brand and you shouldn't take this for granted by using your fans. Give more than you take with your content, always. You can tell people about new products and encourage the sale by following a link, going to the link in your bio on Instagram, or even tapping a link, but don't do this for every single post. You should be giving a lot more than you're taking, especially when you start or if you have a small platform you are trying really hard to grow.

Notes

1. Social Media Today: https://www.socialmediatoday.com/news/the-history-of-social-media-infographic-1/522285/
2. Facebook monthly active users: https://investor.fb.com/investor-events/event-details/2022/Q1-2022-Earnings/default.aspx
3. Instagram users: https://about.instagram.com/about-us
4. Facebook newsroom https://about.fb.com/news/2012/04/facebook-to-acquire-instagram/
5. Pinterest.com https://investor.pinterestinc.com/press-releases/press-releases-details/2022/Pinterest-Announces-Fourth-Quarter-and-Full-Year-2021-Results/default.aspx
6. https://thesmallbusinessblog.net/twitter-statistics/
7. Snapchat active users: https://www.statista.com/statistics/545967/snapchat-app-dau/
8. https://techcrunch.com/2021/12/20/tiktok-to-rank-as-the-third-largest-social-network-2022-forecast-notes/
9. https://about.linkedin.com/

5. Content Marketing

Content, content marketing, content creator; all of these and many others are buzz words at the moment, but when I talk about content marketing here, I'm talking about vlogs and blogs. Social media is, indeed, a form of content marketing but for clarity's sake, it has its own shiny chapter.

Producing content is a great way of promoting you as a brand by providing your potential customers with something of value and ideally something of value that isn't all about the sale.

This doesn't mean that content marketing has no value for making sales, that's absolutely not the case, but it's the way it's done.

Let's say I make a cleaning product for leather. I could write a blog all about my amazing cleaning product, telling you why it's the best product in the world and you'd be mad not to buy it. When I promote this on social, I might use the blog name as part of the caption that would likely be called the name of the product or something similar. Or I could do something else.

I could think about adding value for people through my content and providing information to help them look after their leather really well. How about top tips to care for your leather in the summer? Or how to pick a good leather cleaner? Or five ways to restore dry leather? Each of these pieces of content could:

- help to educate my potential customers
- increase awareness of me as a brand and as an individual
- start to explain why my product is needed
- develop that know–like–trust factor
- help get web traffic if the right keywords are selected and

optimisation used, and that's just the start of it.

Fix a problem

Let's say that 'how to restore dry leather' is what I'm going to write or film about. Through this content, I'll be able to reach people who are having the issue that my product was made to fix, and I'll be able to share the knowledge that I picked up when my product was being developed, for example, along the way.

Maybe dry leather can be nourished faster using a particular kind of grease (that I researched, tested and included in my product). If this is the case, then I could explain a little bit about that, and then when I close the piece stating that one of my products, containing said grease, can be purchased here as the call to action they already know why they need the product.

Isn't blogging a bit old now?

Blogging may seem like its heyday has passed, but I don't think so, especially not when you have the ability, through your blog, to be your own media company. Then there's Google. I'm not an SEO (search engine optimisation) expert but from all the reading I've done (and my own experience of putting these ideas into practice!) Google likes blogs, or at least Google likes fresh content. And more than that, Google helps people find your website when you write blogs around specific content that people are looking for. The blogs have to be good too but that's a whole different subject and something we'll chat about in a moment or two.

Benefits of a blog

As mentioned above, blogging does have its benefits from a techy point of view, but it's so much more than this. When you send a press release into a magazine or copy for an editorial feature, basically anything you do that is not paid for is largely down to luck. You can increase your chances of making the cut significantly (in the ways detailed in that chapter), but, ultimately, you have little control over whether or not the content makes the cut. I'm sorry it's harsh but it's the honest truth. If you pay for an advertorial, of course, you can guarantee this.

Now, you might look at that and think 'why the heck am I wasting my time and energy on something that might never see the light of day?'. It's a good question, and one that a lot of people ask, but one that's not always easy to answer unless you change your thinking slightly.

So, why have I started wittering on about printed media in the Content Marketing chapter? One of the benefits of having a blog is that you can put whatever the heck you like on there. You don't have to get anyone's approval – you can just do it. Yes, your blog may not have tonnes and tonnes of traffic, but if you promote it well and people are interested in what you're talking about, you'll get people reading it. One thing you can publish on your blog is a press release (although I do tend to suggest people go for a slightly adjusted version that's more in their brand voice as there's a difference between a blog and a press release). Adding a press release to your website in this way can be valuable as it allows you to tell the story you want to tell. You wouldn't usually explain how you came up with the idea for a product or service when you were in the shower one day and then you spent ages testing it, things blew up, etc, etc in a product description. You could, but it's not normally a thing (and I don't know what kind of product you've made that keeps blowing up – but there you go!). But what you could do is include a link to the product listing from various places on the blog, and even include a link from the product listing to the blog at the bottom of the product description where people can find out more. Then promote the heck out of it on your social media. You could even put a teaser and link to your blog in your newsletter.

That's just one thing you can put in a blog.

But a blog shouldn't just be about the new products you're trying to sell people. It can be far more than this. Some people view their blog as a journal or their own online magazine, the nature of what you do, the website it sits on and so much more will give you a steer as to the kind of content, but as with all content marketing, don't make everything always about the sale.

Sounds crazy? Hear me out. If you add value to your audience, you're likely to stick in people's minds. You're working on the whole know-like-trust factor that is a really big deal in all types of business. If you give people the chance to know you, what better way than by helping them? You're giving them the opportunity to like you and visit your website or platforms again and ultimately, trust you. Who would you take advice from or buy products from: the person you feel you know? Or the other?

Don't take this to the extreme either and think that I'm saying things don't have to be connected. If you sell sportswear may be writing about the best Victoria Sandwich recipe in the world is a little left field. But you could write about five ways to pick the best running shoes? The best apps for joggers? How to choose a tennis racquet? I'm not overly sporty but you can see where I'm going here, can't you? Not only will this kind of content help to educate your customers (and help them buy the right product or enjoy their sport more), but if you think about the questions your customers are asking, you can link this to the relevant products you sell or add to a frequently asked questions section. If you're really on it, you can think about the SEO on the piece, to help Google show you higher up the search results thus increasing visibility to people who are looking to buy a new pair of running shoes but have no idea where to start.

You don't need anyone's permission to write it or share it or promote it. You can just do it.

How to get started with a blog

If you want to start blogging, you need somewhere to host your work. This might be a blog on your own website or even a website that is, really, only a blog. My blog is part of my website (it just has /blog at the end of my website URL) but, again, this will depend on what you want your blog to achieve for you.

Start with a website

Websites can cost you many thousands, or a bit of time, effort and assistance from your friends Google/YouTube. There are lots of different platforms that provide the framework for a website to be built, such as Wix, Squarespace, Shopify, WordPress etc. I'm not an expert here (I have help from someone who is, don't panic!) but my advice would be to do some research, have a good look around, ask your friends what they use and like, and then go for it.

I use WordPress and have for many years. I bought a theme (there are loads of free ones but the one I liked at the time I did this was paid for – typical!) and then I had a graphic designer do the clever stuff for me. This was a while ago, but I think that theme cost me about $65. The customisation cost quite a lot more because:

I completely changed my mind on EVERYTHING halfway through which meant the work needed to be done twice – I wouldn't advise that

I just didn't believe I could do the customisation. Now, with a few years of using WordPress and making adjustments, I know I could do maybe 80% of the work I had the designer do.

I don't understand code (and you don't need to with most day to day stuff on WordPress), but when I wanted really specific things doing which, in some cases, meant a change to the theme, I needed help. This kind of work was and is way beyond my pay grade (and if you're going down this route and don't know what you're doing, it might be a good call to get a bit of help from a WordPress expert to save your sanity and website). However, in all honestly, I'm SO fussy. The themes (both free and paid for) seem to have come on massively since then, to make them even easier to use. The point is, if you want a basic WordPress website and you're not afraid of searching Google, you'll get a long way.

What's more, you don't need to have a website that could run the planet if you asked it and has all the bells and whistles from the start. You really don't. You just need a platform that you feel is on brand to you. It's amazing what changing colours, fonts, adding your own images and logos can do to make a website feel like yours. It can be the work of a few hours to get yourself up and running with a functional website.

I'm not saying don't use WordPress experts – what I'm saying is that you don't have to. If you get stuck, it's not your bag or you just don't have the time to do it – then don't. There are lots of very able website designers out there who would love to work with you. You can have a Google and search web designers nearby if you'd like that kind of service, or you can pop over to places like People Per Hour, Fiverr and maybe even a Facebook group to find someone who can help you out.

Hosting

One thing to note when you have a blog or a website is that you need somewhere for it to live. A server that it can call home. This is the place that your website and all the code, text and images live and as you'd expect there's more than one way to get this done.

Again, there are different options at different prices starting at free if you make some compromises (one of these is with WordPress, where the name of your website will have wordpress in the URL), or fully managed solutions that can vary in price depending on a number of factors including the size of your website.

It might sound complicated (I buried my head in the sand for a long time about hosting), but it's actually not all that complicated (at least your part of it doesn't have to be) and if you get it wrong, it's actually pretty easy to move (in my experience) too.

Optimum length

As I mentioned above, my website is a WordPress website. One of the benefits of this is that I have a free plugin (a bit of software that you can download to your site to perform a specific function) that 'cheers me on' with various blog writing (it's always nice to have a cheerleader – right?!). This little gem is called Yoast and it's free, although there is a paid for version and this likes each blog post to be over 300 words at least. It's also very keen on longer posts but 300 words is a minimum.

Tim Cameron-Kitchen from Exposure Ninja is an expert on SEO and as blogs are a big part of that, he shares a little wisdom on why blogs need to be a decent length:

> 'Whilst 300 words is a good minimum starting point, the "perfect" length of your blog posts will really depend on the topic. A post answering a question like "what's the weather like in Monaco in October?" might only need 300 words. But something like "How to start a new business" would justify a much longer post – perhaps 3,000 words+.
>
> 'One quick way to see how long a post you should be aiming for is to do a Google search for the blog post topic you're going to be writing about. You can then look through the top-ranking results and see what sort of article lengths Google is already rewarding. If you want to unseat these established posts with your blog post, you'll usually want to provide more detail than the incumbents. We always want to aim to give the searcher a better experience than the alternatives, so that really Google has no choice but to show your website top.
>
> 'If you find that the blog posts ranking for that topic are really detailed and already excellent, you might want to consider niching your topic slightly so that you're competing against weaker posts. It's usually more profitable to hit page 1 for a less competitive term than be on page 5 for a competitive term.'

Although Yoast and, indeed, all the tutorials and how tos would like you to write lengthy posts each time you sit down to type, I would stress that this is largely for SEO. Don't waffle for the sake of it. Because even if you hit the word count you feel you need, if it's utter rubbish that no one is going to read (or not read much of) you're shooting yourself in the foot. The whole point of lovingly writing a blog post is for people to read and enjoy it and ideally that will lead to other things. So, if you manage to get someone to come on over to your blog and you've spent 1000 words telling them something that, really should have taken 200, you're likely to lose them and you don't want that.

A great example of blogs and their varying length is Seth Godin. Seth is basically a legend for all things marketing and he blogs a LOT. Actually, he writes a blog every day. Yes, every day. Some are short, some are long, but they always make a clear point.

Do Seth's blogs rank at the top of Google for everything he's written about? I couldn't tell you, but Seth has such a big tribe of engaged fans that respect, listen to and learn from him, he doesn't need it to. Because the people he wants to communicate with and read his words do. Actually, he encourages people to sign up to his blog so they receive his content each day and some posts aren't even 100 words.

Search engine optimisation (SEO to its friends)

You'll have seen SEO come up a lot in this section and while it's not the only reason to blog (and might not be for you), it can be a nice benefit of sharing your thoughts with the world.

SEO helps to connect your content, your blogs and website, with the people who want to find said content. If you're looking to find out how to hide hashtags on your Instagram Stories, you'll probably find a post I wrote in March 2018 all about it. I didn't write it for this purpose, I wrote it because I wanted to help my followers. But if someone types in that phrase, I'm there.

So what questions are your potential customers asking? Are they wondering how to measure themselves for a product just like yours? Or how to pick the right boot for walking up a mountain in winter? What words and phrases do you want to rank for? The answer isn't just somewhere on Google, be specific, the first page or the top?

There's a bit of an art to SEO, but it can also be quite fun if you apply yourself to it. However, if you can't think of anything worse, it is also something that can be outsourced and you can have help with. Again, it depends on your budget, time and objectives. If you're building a personal brand that's multifaceted and most of your work comes via social media, maybe you'll give it a go yourself. If you have an online business that takes transactions through your website and you can help steer people towards said website for free, why wouldn't you?

Oh yes, that's a key point, SEO works along in the background for free. So, your investment in time or money continues to sit there working for you, long after you press post. SEO results don't happen overnight at all, far from it, but they do work away in the background for you. There's a whole chapter coming up on SEO, but it also felt right to give it a little mention here as it's worth keeping in mind.

Content ideas

Now you have the platform, the hosting, you know the length needed and you have a foundation in SEO and know how it can help you, what the heck do you write about? You could write about anything and you have to pick just one thing and now you can't think of one thing. ARGH!

Relax – I've got you. I love writing (this book is solid evidence of that) so I rarely (up to this point I never have but I'm sure I will at some point so I'm saying rarely) run out of things to write about, so here are a few of my top blog content idea generators to get you going.

Frequently asked questions

I love a Frequently Asked Question, especially one that has a longer answer. An answer I can link to a blog post is heaven. Let me show you some examples.

'How do I find the right size for me?'

This could allow you to create measuring guides in video form, maybe a blog that's a step by step guide with a bullet point list, or maybe even a blog showing different shapes and sizes of people in different sizes to give people an idea of the fit if you sell slim fit, relaxed fit, etc. Actually, if that's the case, you could write a blog called 'what is slim fit?' or 'what's the difference between slim fit and classic fit' if that's what people are asking. You can then link to these from another blog on your relevant product/s, something like: 'We want to make sure your new shirt fits you just perfectly, so we've come up with a step by step guide to ensure you find the shirt that's the right size for you. We also have extra information and lots of images around the different kinds of 'fit' in case you prefer a more snug or more relaxed 'fit'. With links pointing people to those areas.

'How do I clean my jewellery?'

Again, you could create step by step guides as to how to clean jewellery. Or specifically how to clean whatever your jewellery is made from. You could blog about your top cleaning products for the kind of jewellery you sell. Or even your top storage tips for that kind of jewellery to help keep it looking its very best. You could talk about cleaning dips versus polishing cloths. Or natural and eco alternatives. Myths around cleaning types of jewellery. I'm just thinking off the top of my head here.

'What's included in the price of my photoshoot?'

The perfect opportunity to link to your prices page on your website with a detailed list of what each shoot involves, sure, but there's scope for even more here. You could talk about how many images your client is likely to receive from each type of shoot and why it's that number. Or what happens after your shoot, to help show the process from shoot to finished products and it's all included. Maybe it shows the beautiful box the prints come in, or a booklet with ideas for how to show off your new images and framing tips. Not only can this information be so useful to clients, it can actually help you to talk about your unique selling points in a much more open way.

New thoughts and ideas

One thing to blog about is a new product (and above we were talking about repurposing the humble press release), but you can do more than that. Maybe you're an eco-brand and you want to talk about a new law that's been passed, or a new classification, or something that's close to your heart and relevant? Maybe you want to talk about the impact of something in your world? Maybe you have a really strong opinion on something that you have to talk about or else you'll explode. Maybe you have an idea for a new campaign you want to share.

There are so many ideas that could fit into this category that the list could just go on and on, but if it's a new thing, whatever that thing might be, or a thought you want to share, then it's worth considering sharing it on your blog if it's going to strike a chord with your 'tribe'.

Behind the scenes

Not only does behind the scenes content make incredible blog content, but it performs really well on social media too, because these snippets you're providing are extra special.

Don't worry, you don't need to give away all your trade secrets and, more to the point, you don't need to share anything you don't want to, but even being aware of this as a concept when you're developing an idea is a good call.

So, for example, let's say you're making a new product. Maybe you take people along with you on your journey either at the time (if you can) or when you're launching the product and you can tell them more. Maybe you can talk about the design process and show some drawings and even prototypes that you made along your journey? Maybe you interview some of the artisans or team members that help you bring your ideas to life? Maybe you take people along on the photoshoot and document it all so people get a look behind the lens too. Then there's the packaging, people's first reactions, packing up orders. There's a lot you can do and this is just with a product!

You can also take people behind the scenes with the day to day running of your business. From the office dog to what fuels your office (as in cake/biscuits/tea rather than electricity/oil), celebrating special events together and what they mean, your team... I could go on and on. But the key thing here to note is that the things you experience each day in your business are not 'normal' to others. The way you gift wrap could turn into a masterclass, the head of accounts could have passions and beliefs that your fans and followers connect with, the books that helped you get to where you are today could inspire something in someone else, etc.

When you're thinking about behind the scenes, you need to think outside of yourself and look at what you do and how this might be interesting to someone who has never experienced it before. The skills you have developed in running your business or developing the traits that have allowed you to build your personal brand are interesting. Don't undervalue that. If you need a little help seeing them, then ask a friend or even ask your fans and followers on social media.

Guest blogs

Oh – this is gold dust! Getting fans, customers and other personal brands and brands who align with you to guest blog has so many benefits. First up, if you're struggling with content or can't think of another way to look at an issue, they're likely to be able to assist you, but more than that, all the stuff we've been talking about above? They can bring their own spin on it to the table. How good is that?

When someone guest blogs for you, you want to make sure that you do a good job for them – and this means you need to really think of why you've asked them or accepted their request and nurture that. That way you're likely to get the best out of them and bring something new and different to your website and blog readers.

Let's say you're a fashion brand who makes a range of dresses and Jane, who's big on social for her understanding of make-up and tutorials, says that she'd like to guest blog for you. Brilliant. But don't make Jane write about your clothing exclusively. Yes, maybe there's a way you can incorporate your products (like the perfect smoky eye for nights out – cue images of one of your dresses on Jane with said product, or in an image of Jane and her stunning eye make-up with the products used), or what colour lipstick to wear with red, but don't make her write just about your products. Harness what she's good at.

Another nifty way to work with others is by sending people who you'd like to feature a list of questions. You might want to adjust a few questions for each person who receives this, but through the list you're ensuring that you have the guest blogger's information that you can share (like social media handles) as well as information about them that allows people to get to know them a bit better. Depending on your brand, you might find a combination of serious and more light-hearted questions work, but you can also weave in questions that support what they do.

Let's go back to Jane and our dress business. Maybe you'd ask Jane about the lipstick colour, but maybe you'd ask a fashion photographer for a top tip when it comes to posing for mirror selfies on Instagram? Maybe you'd ask a beautician about winter nail colours that are hot this season. Maybe you'd ask them all for their go-to little black dress/the favourite dress they've ever worn and why... see where I'm going here? You want to tap into them, their essence, to provide real value.

When you do this, you're much more likely to find that the bloggers will actively promote their feature on your website to their following (especially if you make it easy for them to do this) as they're proud of what they have done for you and you've let them be themselves in a way that will really appeal to their audience.

Another benefit of guest blogs is you often have the opportunity to guest blog right back, meaning that you can get in front of their audience again, in a different way.

With all collaborations, everyone has to benefit, so just keep this in mind when you're working out how to work with someone like this.

A word about blogs

They are not, repeat not, product descriptions. Your product descriptions should be product descriptions and your blogs should bring something else to the party. Think of your blog more like a place for articles for your brand's own magazine. The tone will be different (most likely it'll be chattier and more personal) and more engaging to read. You can link to your relevant products too, that's fine, actually, my little blog plugin gives me a green light when I add internal links. It's good like that.

Vlogs

Vlogs, a combination of video and blog, are also great ways to document what you're up to and share it with the world. Unlike feature length films, vlogs don't need to be polished and perfect, the joy is that they're meant to show real life. Or at least the real life you're happy to share. What's more, unlike a few years ago, you don't need to buy any kit to start vlogging (well, I'm assuming you have a smartphone with video recording functionality here), you just need your phone. Maybe download an editing app too, but it's all in the palm of your hand.

Video is the future

Video is the future. If you hate video as much as I know some people do, I'm genuinely sorry to say this but it is, it really is. I'm going to look at some of the most popular places to put your videos in just a moment, but for now I want to talk about video as a whole.

According to Google, six out of ten people would rather watch online video than TV.[1] 74% of marketers say that video has a better return on investment than a static image.[2] If you search on Google you'll find lots of other impressive video marketing facts.

If you're not comfortable with video, you're not going to enjoy this section but please stick with it.

YouTube

A section about vlogs that doesn't include YouTube is, well, not a strong section in my honest opinion. But that might just be me. Not only does YouTube have some incredible stats that show its rise in, well, everything, it has also created some incredible stars: Zoella, Alfie Deyes, to name but two. YouTube has the most amazing scope.

I promised you some YouTube stats, didn't I? These are all taken from the horse's mouth so to speak, as in YouTube, in May 2022:[3]

- over two billion logged in users visit per month
- one billion hours of YouTube content are watched EACH

DAY.

There are more stats (there are always more, aren't there?) and these continue to be mind-blowing. But when it comes to where to host your video content, you've got to consider it.

In addition to the incredible amount of users, YouTube also works well for your SEO if you optimise your headers, description, etc, is very searchable (it's actually the second largest search engine in the world behind Google according to some websites – and I can believe it – if I need to fix anything or learn how to do something, you know where I go!? YouTube!), and you can embed the YouTube videos into your own blog or website too, giving your videos greater exposure.

Facebook videos

Facebook might be the place you put your images, thoughts, graphics and more, but it's also a great place to upload your videos, straight into Facebook.

So why would you do this? There are a few reasons why I think you need to consider it.

- the video is displayed in an inviting way that encourages people to click
- if enabled, videos uploaded to Facebook auto play and a video can be mesmerising and scroll stopping in equal measure
- you can subtitle videos inside Facebook with ease (and a lot of people watch Facebook videos on silent so that's a useful function)
- there are other things you can do to encourage views that can really help to increase interest and engagement
- you can boost it to your followers or targeted groups of

people on Facebook.

There are more reasons too. New features and functions are being introduced ALL THE TIME, so while you might pick this up, read it, and agree with all of the above (here's hoping), you may have also found a new function that will allow you to get even more views.

Instagram video

The newest kid of the video block, Instagram Video, formerly Instagram TV or IGTV really came into its own when you could share a preview on your main feed. Because that, to me, meant everything joined up and worked as one platform rather than two.

Instagram Video came onto the scene as a platform designed to honour the mobile user. Sounds a bit far-fetched? Think of YouTube, the videos it displays are landscape which means that in order to see the full picture, you need to turn your phone 90 degrees to make it landscape, at which point the whole screen will fill with the video you're watching. Instagram Video doesn't need turning, its videos are made to be viewed in portrait.

When it was IGTV originally, landscape videos simply didn't work on it, but then a change was announced that would allow landscape videos to work on the platform, but in portrait. This meant that you'd have big borders at the top and bottom if you uploaded without editing. We've mentioned 'scroll stopping' content a few times, and the big borders didn't help catch people's attention and didn't necessarily stop the scroll.

However, while Stories will only show 15 second clips, Video allows you to post much longer videos, provides a place to keep your live content long after you've signed off, and can feature on your main grid too. This, to me, makes Instagram Video a really valuable tool. Because producing a video takes a lot of time and energy and you want your masterpiece to be seen. And to me sharing on Instagram is the perfect way to do this.

Short form video

I couldn't write about video without mentioning short form video. By this, I mean video that lasts just a few short seconds but has the ability to capture attention, deliver a message, entertain, shock and anything else in between. Many platforms have short form video. TikTok is known for it and it's arguably where it all started, but YouTube now has Shorts, and Instagram has Reels. Although these videos are short in length (usually just a few seconds but can be over a minute depending on the platform), don't discard them. They can pack a serious punch and have the ability to go viral. You need to be creative in how you get your point across so quickly, but this doesn't need to be difficult. Audio is also a huge part of most short form videos with lip syncing, transitions in time to music and dancing are becoming more popular to keep that attention and encourage engagement.

These shorter videos are really popular at the time of writing this book, and I would urge you to give them a go. Look at what others are doing, but don't let it overwhelm you as most of the videos we see are actually very simple if you break them down.

Where to put your video

If you can't decide where to put your video, don't panic. If you like you can put your video in all the places. If you don't want to edit or shoot two videos, you will need to consider the format. I would base this on either where I wanted to get the most views and subscribers or where I had the most subscribers/the largest audience to go after. And then make it in that format.

If you don't really mind and just want the views then go for where you have the biggest engaged audience, but I wouldn't discount the other places. I wouldn't, however, release the same video on all the platforms at the same time on the same day. Spread the joy, OK?

Content inspiration

You might be chomping at the bit to get cracking and then start to realise you're a little lighter on content ideas than you'd like. Don't worry, I have some below. But the key thing you have to remember is you need to just start. Your first one, when you look back on it, won't be your best. But you have to record and post this first video to allow yourself to grow. Without it, you won't really get the impact that the light can have, or the wind, or the value of breathing when you're talking to camera, or so many other things. You've got to start. The good news is that with a phone you have all you need to get cracking.

So, if you're stuck for ideas, revisit the blog ideas above but also consider...

- behind the scenes
- weekly updates
- events
- day in the life
- new things/products/services, etc.

Don't be afraid to look at YouTube for inspiration. Look at videos in your niche and see what subjects they're covering, how popular they are, and if you can do your take on the video. Do not copy others, it's not good, but by being aware of what people want, you can make content that they have an interest in watching and you want that.

Notes

1. https://www.thinkwithgoogle.com/marketing-strategies/video/ video-trends-where-audience-watching
2. Biteable https://biteable.com/blog/video-marketing-statistics
3. https://blog.youtube/press/

6. Collaboration Potential

Collaborations are where it's at on so many things. Yes, there's a bit more work involved in contrast to when you go it alone, but the rewards can be much greater and it can be much more fun too.

Collaborations in the content area can take many forms, and you'll no doubt have seen a few as you've been browsing the internet. Guest blogs are a really simple way to collaborate, where someone who has relevant knowledge or something key to share that your fans and followers would appreciate writes something for you, and ideally you reciprocate. You don't always have to write for each other when it comes to guest blogging, but I do feel that in the true nature of collaboration, it's good.

Another idea for a collaboration would be something involving video. So maybe you interview someone for a video you're planning to put on YouTube, Instagram or Facebook and they do something similar (or maybe something completely different but it should still give you exposure to their audience). Sometimes video collabs can be a bit more awkward due to geographical location, but I've also seen this work across continents. I remember watching a 'hack' style video (as in, where people share their clever little ways to get around life's issues or events) and one YouTuber did five hacks, and another did five, on different videos. Actually, different videos on different channels. I thought it was a fun yet really simple idea. It was in the mummy blogger space, so realistically if you're following a lady with three children and you're interested in how she manages them, you could well be interested in another lady who is in the same situation. I actually thought the cross-continent thing was quite fun as it's always good to see how different people do different things, isn't it?

Of course, a collaboration does not simply end with the creation of the content, oh no, the promotion of said collaboration is key and that's definitely something to consider.

Let's get into collaborations

At the end of the last chapter, I talked about collaborations as part of your content marketing strategy, but collaborations can be so much bigger than this and so diverse too. There's no one size fits all when it comes to collaborations, and as we wander through this chapter together, I would like you to use what you find here to guide and inspire you rather than serve as a list of hard and fast rules that must be obeyed and never deviated from. That's just not fun.

Before we go any further, I want you to keep something in mind about collaborations. I always say that when you collaborate, both or all depending on how many people you collaborate with should win. If one person doesn't, it's not really a collaboration, it's more being taken advantage of.

Why collaborate?

When you collaborate, lots of things can happen, but the main reason to start is the exposure to a new audience. By working with people who share some of your character traits, passions, interests, hobbies, taste in music, whatever you've decided your brand is, you're likely to find that some people in their audience might be interested in you and vice versa.

Of course, it does depend who you collaborate with, but be in no doubt that the right collaborations can be mega and do huge things for your brand and following as it's getting you in front of new relevant people. It's more than just an ad, it's putting some context behind it. So rather than 'this is Jo, she likes horses, you should follow her' as an ad may seem, a good collaboration would provide relatable insight, information or tips that would show that Jo was actually a very accomplished horsewoman who others could gain a lot from following.

See the difference? I don't know about you, but I'm getting more and more picky about the people I spend my time with (online and offline) and I want to make sure I'm spending the time I spend staring at my screens well, so if someone I follow and trust is giving me good reason to follow and engage with someone they trust, I'm likely to take that a lot more seriously.

What's the cost?

I wouldn't say 'the best bit is...' because the right collaborations can yield a ton of best bits, but one of the best bits about well thought through collaborations is that they can cost you nothing or very little. The differential comes in the kind of brand you have and what you're planning to do together.

Of course, I'm not saying 'don't spend anything on your collaboration', but what I'm saying is that with a good pinch of creativity and hard work you have the potential to create something pretty spectacular for no actual money. You'll need to spend time on your collaboration, whatever form that takes and you might want to throw a few pounds behind a Facebook ad to boost it a little, but the entry cost to get started is zilch. How exciting is that?

It's hard work, right?

Generally, I find you can either throw money at a problem to fix it OR you can throw time at it. There are very few amazing things that happen without some kind of input – short of winning the lottery. But don't let this put you off. Depending on the nature of the collaboration, you might find the work really good fun (that's kind of part of the joy of it), you might learn new skills, find new friends, grow your network, any number of things. All while working to increase your reach, audience and following.

How can you collaborate?

When it comes to the how, the list is pretty much endless, you make your collaboration whatever you like. This will likely depend on the kind of audience you have. But here are a few ideas. As I said at the top of the chapter, please don't use this as a list of things you can never deviate from. I want you to innovate, take a seed of an idea and let it grow and grow into something incredible – OK? And when you've done this, please tag me on Instagram or Facebook and tell me what you've done, I really do LOVE this kind of thing!

So, some ideas for how:

1. Guest blogs – we chatted about this in the previous chapter, so maybe have a re-read if you need a refresh.
2. Interviews – a bit like a guest blog but more prescriptive. Maybe you can take this a step further and ask your audience what they'd like to ask your interviewee? To get a real community feel going for the interview. Maybe you could write, record and film your interview? The great thing with an interview is that you can make it as fun or as

serious as you like, or maybe even a mixture of the two if you fancy it.
3. Collaborative vlogs – again, pop back and have a look at some ideas around this subject.
4. Competitions – these can be really good and as there are quite a few things to consider, we're exploring this in more detail.

Competitions

Competitions are a great way to collaborate. Not only are they really simple to organise, but it's not just the people who collaborate who 'win', oh no, their audiences do too.

I often run competitions connected to the podcasts I record, and I sometimes do them as completely standalone competitions connected to an event that's going on, a specific day, or something else. Sometimes, when I run the competition around a podcast, a product or service will be donated or given for me to giveaway to my fans and followers. These work so well.

For me they work well because I've been given something to give away, that I can use to promote the podcast I've produced and, therefore, promote the guest, but if someone has given something as a prize, they're likely to promote it to their audience too. When this happens, things can take on a life of their own.

Competitions and social media

The competitions I'm talking about above are run through social media. This isn't the only place you can run a competition, but at the time of writing I would wager that that's one of the easiest ways to do it.

Now, social media competitions are good if you want to gain more exposure to potential fans, but they don't do a whole lot for your mailing list, for example, so make sure you think about what you want to gain from your competition. If you want to grow your mailing list, then although you would promote your competition through social media, you would move the entry mechanism away from social (and comply with all relevant data rules, of course). But we're going to assume that you want to increase your reach and exposure here and that's relevant to the next bit.

Follow the rules

Ah rules – what's that saying, 'rules make games fun'? I kind of subscribe to that idea, although a lot of the world doesn't!

Each social media platform has a set of Terms and Conditions of use and when you want to use them to run a competition, you really need to make sure you understand that section of the Ts and Cs. Search 'promotion guidelines for...' and away you go. I run most competitions on Facebook and Instagram and even though they're owned by the same company, the Ts and Cs are different. People regularly break the rules when running giveaways on these platforms and that's on them (and really, REALLY annoys the people who try and play by the rules), but it's on you what you do. Please have a read of what you're meant to do (and not meant to do) before you decide.

In addition to the Ts and Cs of the platform and how you're allowed to run a competition connected to these, there are the wider terms and conditions too. This is not an exhaustive list at all, but you need to make sure you're really clear about everything you can be. Exactly what the prize is, whether there are any geographical or age limits on the winner, the closing date, etc. Again, this isn't the full list, but it's a place to start and a place you can build from.

One final word on this type of collaboration – in my experience simplicity wins. I've seen a lot of competitions on social media over the years. Some you've needed a degree to even enter. Others it takes you mere moments. I often give up with the hard ones. When I need to follow a million accounts, then join a mailing list, then share, then tag, then stand on one leg (OK, never had this before) I give up because no one wants a bottle of shampoo THAT much! Think about your objective and try to keep one, just one, in mind for each competition. This will allow you to clearly decide the entry mechanism and how fewer steps you can limit the entry process to. Please do this. For your sake and your entrants' sake. Because don't forget that if they need to do a million things in order to enter, you need to make sure that they have done a million things to be a valid entry and maybe winner. Because if you can't, it's not fair on them (for whatever they've had to do at great time cost to them) OR the people who entered. Sometimes the functions that we ask people to do are incredibly difficult to track. Or at least they're time consuming when mixed with the rest of your list. Just one clear objective means you can pick the easiest way to enter, which will get you to your desired goal too. If you want the entry to be super simple, it's more likely that people will share and tell their friends, and, you know, actually enter in the first place!

Collaboration tips

Some important tips to keep in mind:

- you should both be in it to benefit each other as well as

yourself
- you should have shared interests that will translate in your content
- your audiences should appreciate the collaboration and understand why it's being shown to them
- you should both work on the promotion of said collaboration
- if one person has a much greater following, the one with the smaller following may have to deliver more in some areas, but that's very easily solvable.

Try it. Seriously. The best way to see if a collaboration is going to work is by doing your checks (as above) and then cracking on. If it's something like a guest blog the only real commitment is a bit of time and if it doesn't work out, you could always repurpose that for your own means. Also, if it doesn't work out, you'll know why and this could be different for each person. Maybe you're someone who needs more structure, for example? That could be something to keep in mind when you try again. You'll learn when it doesn't work out and if it does work out, you'll gain and learn, so there's nothing to lose!

7. Influencers, Brand Ambassadors and Sponsored People

Not sure what the difference between influencers, brand ambassadors and sponsored people are? Worry not, in this chapter I'll be giving it all a pretty serious airing. But let's start with the basics. Well, the basics as I see it anyway.

An influencer is someone who usually uses social media and/or blogs and has a following that they have influence over.

A brand ambassador is a specific person, often an influencer, that a brand has asked to become an ambassador for them. This usually involves being more exclusive with the kind of content an influencer shares or wears in a specific and connected area. Sometimes money changes hands, sometimes it's product only.

A sponsored person is usually someone a company pays to support and therefore, work with. Again, this can be payment in product or money. There will be an attribute to said sponsored person that makes them appeal to the company, but it might not be connected to their social media or personal brand. It might be connected to their sporting prowess, for example.

Is this a trend?

Sponsorship has been around for a long time, especially in sport. To be able to compete (and win) at a high level, athletes have to dedicate a huge amount of time to their sport and passion. In addition to needing the time to hone their skills and keep improving, many require expensive equipment, training and so much else.

All this costs money and often a lot of it.

By working with companies in a sponsored way, the sponsored person can receive support to help them achieve this goal and, in exchange, the company gets credit as a sponsor in various different ways. Some of these sponsorships and partnerships are nothing short of incredible. They support people in achieving their goals, in some cases winning medals and representing their country too. In return, the company enjoy the exposure and feel good of being part of that journey. Maybe they get perks they can extend to their clients like hospitality, exclusive access, etc. You get the idea. This isn't new.

According to campaignlive.co.uk, branding connected to a sponsor first appeared on a football shirt in 1976. In the grand scheme of things this is a particularly long time but things do seem to have accelerated at an incredible pace. Just a look down Forbes' highest paid athletes list shows how much money some of these athletes earn from their sponsors. And generally, the better and more well known the athlete, the larger than amount of money a sponsor is willing to pay for that association.

Now, in the olden days (how old am I?!), sponsorship was connected to a skill, usually a sport. Now the skill can be being popular. Simple as that. Sharing your lifestyle, your parenting style, how to make slime, how you apply make-up, all of these things and so many more can help you grow a big following online. And that makes you valuable for a brand. Because you have the ability to get their brand of clothes/baby food/slime ingredients/make-up in front of people interested in said products and looking to buy them. That has a value.

The thing is, the value can be considerably more than traditional media in terms of exposure.

Let's start with influencers

Unless you've been living under a rock, I'm in no doubt that you will have heard the term influencer before. This is more than likely if you use social media and have a small business, you've seen it and heard it again and again. Maybe you've even used it. Heck, maybe you are one?

The truth is that anyone and everyone who uses social media has the power to influence others. And that's actually very exciting. However, the term 'influencer' is usually applied to people with a significant following on social media, although that's not always the case.

Different types of influencer

While I'm saying that there are different types of influencer, that isn't entirely accurate, it's more like there are different levels of influencer. The higher the 'level' in this ranking, generally, the higher the follower number. This means, assuming that this following has been built correctly and organically, that the influencer has more influence because more people are seeing the content they put out.

You with me?

Now, the main thing about this that will impact you, whether you are an influencer with a significant engaged following or the brand looking to work with the influencer, is that the bigger the following, the more you can charge OR the more you're likely to pay to work with said influencer.

If you're a brand looking to work with an influencer, you might smart at this idea (and if you aren't, well done you, it's not worth it), but hear me out. If you were looking to advertise in a magazine, one of the figures you would look at would be the circulation of the magazine. If a magazine has a circulation of 1000 people, you are likely to pay less than a magazine with a circulation of 1000000 people. Because more eyeballs are seeing your advert and, therefore, the greater the chance of a conversion (in this example just assume it's exactly the same audience). It's the same with an influencer, although there is a caveat in there too and why there's a real trend towards micro influencers.

Anyone who has a sizable social media account will know that it takes some upkeep. Not only the posting but also the commenting to get that all important engagement, the DMs, etc. Now, when you have a smaller account, it's much easier to keep on top of this and nurture that engagement. The kind of engagement that is likely to lead to conversions and sales. Simply because you can. As your account grows and gets bigger and bigger, you would not have enough hours in the day to be able to pay your million followers the same amount of care and attention as someone with a thousand followers. This isn't a criticism; it's maths and life. Now, because of this, while a big influencer can reach more people, a micro one has the ability to form greater connections with less, thus making a conversion more likely because they have been able to give one to one time to that essential know-like-trust equation.

How to assess an influencer

The next bit feels more focussed on brands wishing to work with influencers, but if you're on a quest to grow your influencer credentials and want to make yourself a whole lot more attractive to brands, the below might be of use to you too.

There are many different ways that you can assess an influencer at the start. Here's what I look at.

1. Their follower number – just for a rough idea to see what kind of bracket the influencer I'm looking at is in.
2. Their engagement – which is actually more important than point one as following without engagement in my experience isn't useful to me or the brands I work with.
3. Their tone – how do they talk to their fans and followers; does it align with your brand?
4. Their interests and following connected to this – again, does this align with your brand?
5. Their consistency – are they actively using social media or just as and when the mood takes them?
6. The quality of the content – what do their images, videos, captions and words look and read like? Are they good? Will it work for you and your audience?

If you look at this list, you will be able to secure a list of potentials. But a word of warning here – do the groundwork. Don't just look at the last few posts and think you've done a good job and you can move on with your life. Look back further. You don't have to go back to the beginning of time but scroll on back and just see where they started. Firstly, it's nice to see someone's journey and how they've developed as a brand, but you'll also get to find out so much more about them, their passions, their interests and their beliefs if you scroll back, and this can help inform your decision about whether or not you want to work with them.

The thing is that if you pick the wrong ambassador, you're both going to have a bad day at the office and I don't want that for either of you.

The steps above won't mean you'll never ever make a mistake, I'm not a magician and can't guarantee such things, sadly. But I would say it's a good start to limiting these mistakes. As you start to observe, you will see things that really matter to you as a brand. Maybe, I don't know, there are pictures on a potential influencer's grid of them drinking heavily and that turns out to be a big no for you because your audience are children, for example. Well that would then become a 'deal breaker' or a standalone point to consider and this will make the process much easier for you.

Now what?

Let's say you have a shortlist of potential influencers you might like to work with. Exciting, hey? Now you watch and comment. Engage with their content. It might sound boring and you may well be chomping at the bit here, but there are at least two benefits: you get to know them better and they get to know you better. The latter is as important as the former.

Influencers with a big following can charge serious money for exposure to their audience. If you're going in with a big hitter, you want to make sure that they're a good fit because you will need to put your money where your mouth is, but you also need them to want to work with you. If they're doing everything right they're likely to be receiving a few offers and unlike magazines who can sell a lot of advertising in each issue, influencers can't do this. They have a finite amount of time (even with a team) and their audience will have a certain amount of attention. They will have other projects on the go too so they need to make sure that the associations they make are right for them.

This is where you can win by watching and engaging, see? Because SOCIAL media is about relationships and connections. If you learn how the influencer likes to work, the kind of projects that they go for, the support the brand gives to the influencer, etc, when you approach them, you're likely to do so with something that's going to work for them. That increases your chances of a yes, but it also increases your chances of a 'no, but in the future yes'. If you approach a vegan with your amazing beef burgers that come through the post, no one is getting on board with that. They'll think you've just picked them because of the number under their name and you'll be blacklisted. Seriously. Don't.

If you start to engage with the content and learn what they do and what works for them, they'll also get to see you. When people see you, when you approach them and say you've been enjoying their content and loved their trip to Venice – that shot with the gelato at sunset was your favourite – they'll know you've been watching and caring. As we're dealing with people, this matters.

I know when I get approached by brands to work with them, I want to see that they have shown some interest in what I'm doing. They don't need to know my inside leg measurement, but nothing makes me say no quicker than someone who has no understanding of what makes me tick. Because, really, where can we go from there? With the influencers I advise and work with, they say 'no' far more than they say 'yes'.

How much will it cost you?

This depends on so many factors. In some cases, it'll cost you product. In some cases, it'll cost you product and money. Generally, the larger the following the more of everything you'll need to throw at the situation.

The pricing isn't solely limited to size of following though. It depends what you want for the product or money.

Lots of brands gift items to influencers. Some send to big influencers via PO Box in the hope of getting featured on social should the influencer love the product. This can work really well if the above comes true but can equally be like throwing your product into the sea if the influencer doesn't like it or gives it away.

Sometimes a brand can gift and an ambassador accepts on the loose condition that if they like the product they will feature it at some point on their social media. There's no minimum amount of posts or times or any form of control by the brand. But usually the price to get involved with this would be product based.

Now we step up a gear. If you're asking for a certain number of posts a week or month you may have to back up the gifted products with money. If you want control over the content then you're in fully fledged ad territory and that's likely to warrant a price tag.

Just one teeny note here, it's worth brushing up on your ASA (Advertising Standards Agency) and CMA (Competition & Markets Authority) guidelines regarding working with influencers and what they need to declare. Basically, they need to be totally transparent with their audience at all times but I really think they should be anyway, regardless of the rules, it's just common decency, so please support this. If you search 'ASA Influencer Guidelines' on your favourite search engine, you'll find the information.

Any influencer worth their salt won't work with you if they don't like what you do and wouldn't spend their own money on it. It's not fair on their audience if they're telling them something is great when secretly they hate it. If you work with someone and they don't get your product at all, don't make them say something untrue, please, it's not good for anyone. The credibility that attracted you to that influencer has now been destroyed too. No one wins here.

Brand ambassadors

If we draw a Venn diagram of all influencers, brand ambassadors and sponsored people, there is a point where they all cross and a point where brand ambassador and influencer overlap too. So, as you read on, don't think 'hang on, that sounds like an influencer' because it probably does!

As I see it, there are a few differences between brand ambassadors and straight up influencers. One is that a brand ambassador is usually connected to a brand for more than one product or campaign, and secondly that a brand ambassador doesn't necessarily need to have influence on social media or to the masses. The relationship can be quite different. Of course, there are other differences too, but I thought addressing those straight up was a good idea.

Let's start with talking about brand loyalty. When I'm looking at people with my brand ambassador shortlisting hat on, brand loyalty matters a lot. If the person, let's call her Mollie, doesn't seem to have a favourite brand in the space I'm working in, that's one thing, if she sings the praises of a competitor's brand all the time, she's not the ambassador for me. Because to me, you want your ambassador to already be cheerleading for you before you ask them to work with you on a more exclusive basis. Why? Because if they're flag waving when they're paying for something, they're much more likely to deliver when they're being gifted items. Also, for their audience, it makes sense. Sticking by a brand they have been raving about forever and getting more involved makes perfect sense. It's a nice transition that fans and followers can get behind and support. The kind of support you want.

If you were following someone who was constantly singing the praises of a particular make of boot, let's say and had been for ages, you'd quite rightly assume that they liked that boot and were sharing their genuine love with you. Now imagine the next day there are no more mentions of that boot and everything is about a conflicting brand. Everything. I'm not saying that they buy a new pair of boots and it's different and they chat about it and take you through the process, I'm talking about 0-60 in the boot praise game. What would you think? Would you think that they maybe hadn't put the effort in and were perhaps being a little less than authentic so they could receive free boots?

This isn't to say that once someone has declared their love for a brand that's them done for life, absolutely not, but there's usually a kind of process. If you're a brand reading this thinking 'but I really wanted to approach x about being a brand ambassador for me but they love another brand so I can't', just hold your horses for a minute. The sharp transition is what will spook people, in my experience. But you don't have to go from zero to brand ambassador in one step and I'd suggest you don't, even with an avid fan.

If you have someone in your sights as a brand ambassador, you need to start to nurture that relationship with them. To engage with their content and to get a feel for what they're all about and what makes them tick. Then, what I would suggest, would be gifting an item to them. If this is an avid fan of your brand, gift them a new product and see what they do with it. They already know your brand values and they should know their audience, so work with them on the exact product, but maybe give them the chance to try something new. If it's someone who doesn't have an affinity to the brand, put the time in and see what might work for them, that is, if they're interested in working with you. If you're looking at someone with the long game in mind, encourage them to put the product through its paces before they share anything with their audience. It's not right for someone to get something like a pair of shoes, take them out of the box and proclaim that they are clearly the best shoes in the whole world when they haven't so much as tried them on.

This doesn't necessarily mean you don't get any coverage for months, but we're playing the long game here and a quick win could really hurt that. Maybe you could encourage them to share an unboxing video or photo and their first impressions and to explain that they've been encouraged to put the product to the test. If it's the kind of product that takes a while to be effective like a cream for example, give them time to make sure they like it. If you want to work with someone long term, see this 'investment' in product and time as a punt. A calculated one but thinking of it like this it might help.

Often, influencers will work with a number of similar brands if they want to, but brand ambassadors usually don't, so while you might treat them the same in some ways, the long term relationship is the focus and that will take time to build but can reap huge rewards.

The role of a brand ambassador is a little different to a standard influencer as although you might have specific pushes around key campaigns, you would expect them to like the brand and products enough that items were incorporated into their life anyway. That's why it's good to work with people who are genuine fans. Because they're probably already doing this. There are lots of benefits to this, an obvious big one being that if they're active on social media and post images or stories of themselves regularly, you're likely to see your product popping up here, there and everywhere, which is always nice. You might also find that your brand ambassador can help with other things you do. Maybe you run or attend events where a little extra support is needed on the ground? Maybe you need roving reporters at events to help get your social media content? Maybe you need models for a photoshoot and they're up for it?

Brand ambassadorships can be incredibly collaborative if handled correctly and if you have an active ambassador who wants to make a name for themselves, build a personal brand and is knocking it out of the park for you, help them. This doesn't mean you have to dedicate masses of time to helping their quest for fame at the expense of your own, but just thinking about little ways you could give them a leg up can be massive. Maybe sharing their images and properly tagging and crediting them (with permission obviously) on your sizable platform would help? Working with them on a giveaway to promote themselves? Encouraging people to follow them. Talking to your friend who just so happens to own a business that would be the most perfect match for your ambassador (and doesn't conflict with yours, of course) can help.

As I mentioned above, brand ambassadors don't have to be amazing on social media. Nowadays they often are, but they don't HAVE to be if that's not a must for you. Yes, it makes sense for them to have influence in some circles, but (depending on your niche) these circles might not be on social media, or not just on social media alone. You might have someone who's a real mover and shaker amongst your target market in real life, who loves what you do. They might be a perfect brand ambassador even if their social media is lacking. Maybe this person will be 'working the floor' wearing whatever you sell and you can use them for photoshoots or something else. We're thinking long term here.

If you're reading this thinking 'yes, that's what I need, I need a brand ambassador', here's a quick checklist to help you find the right one for you.

1. Do they know and like/love your brand? If they have bought from you and are singing the praises of what you do when they have handed over their hard earned cash, they should at least make it into the 'maybe' pile.
2. Do they represent a direct competitor? Obviously if they are an ambassador for a competitor the chances of you working with them immediately are reduced. This doesn't mean you can never approach them as we never know the intricacies of an agreement from the outside, so don't rule them out totally.
3. How many brands do they work with? You don't want someone who collects brands for sport, as the chances of them being able to do a good job for all of these brands isn't high.
4. Look for loyalty. Look at their feed, how they interact with the brands they work with, what brands they use, and how often they switch between them and you'll get an idea.
5. Does their following align with your brand and messaging? Are their beliefs aligned? Look at their content and their fans/followers to check this.
6. Do you know them well? Start to engage with them and get to know them better. If this person is going to be out there waving the flag for your brand it's really important.
7. Don't expect miracles overnight. Give them time to find their stride. See what they do with a product that you gift

to them. Explain it's a gift and don't put them under any pressure because you'll learn more by watching what they do than you will from orchestrating the whole thing. Also, if they do become a brand ambassador, you don't want to be micromanaging them. You've picked them because they tick boxes for you, you don't need to be spending your valuable time stressing about what they have or haven't done every second. Of course, you can offer guidance and chat to them if they ask, but it's getting into the specifics that I would really avoid at this stage. See what they do. They should be looking to work with you in a way that works for them and their audience, and you'd do well to watch, absorb and learn.

8. Accept that you'll make the wrong call sometimes. You can do everything and more but sometimes things just don't work out. This is life. Accept it and move on as quickly as you can. This should allow you to part on good terms and you'll learn a lot of lessons too.

If your trial works then you have the scope to move on. There are lots of different ways that you can work with brand ambassadors and this very much depends on your product, service or industry, and I would urge you to find your own way here to make it work for you, but do also look at what others do in your space. You don't need to do the same but if you know what's normal, you can innovate around this, knowing you have a firm platform. And obviously speak to your brand ambassador or potential brand ambassador too. If they have a full-time job, a hectic home life, or a squillion things to do, you might find they're going to offer you a lot less time and exposure than someone with has a slightly more 'sedate' life. This doesn't mean you shouldn't use the super busy one, but you look at what might work for them and tailor your offer accordingly.

In my experience, most brand ambassadors are 'paid' with

product, especially when it comes to small businesses working with brand ambassadors, but that doesn't mean it has to be that way. You do what works for you. Again, it will depend on factors like industry, product, content produced and ambassador, but really think about what you'd like and what they can deliver. And come to an agreement. Because there's no point saying you want a video a week if the person is absolutely terrified of video. You simply won't get the content or the ambassador will hate every second of its creation and hate you a little bit as a consequence. You don't want that.

Agreements and contracts

This is down to you. I'm not a solicitor so I'm not going to say whether or not you should have a contract as it does depend on so many factors, one major one would be the investment on your part. If you're loaning someone a car, you want to make sure that ambassador has signed on the dotted line. If you're giving a product worth a few pounds, then that might be different, or it might not be to you. I'd suggest getting legal advice on this if you are unsure.

What I can say from experience though, is that some kind of agreement is a good call as it just manages expectations. This can be as simple as an email outlining the 'rules' of how you're going to work together. This is a new area of marketing, so the rules aren't well known and they aren't the same for everyone. One brand might be incredibly strict with what they need even down to the layout of a blog post, image size and word count, another might ask for a tag on Instagram when a relevant post is shared. Some agreements may include how much that person will get paid per month for the content you need and others might offer gifted items as and when and a hefty discount off anything else.

Whatever path you pick, work with your brand ambassador on the ins and outs. You want to manage expectations. You want to give the brand ambassador the best chance of success and you want to do your best to ensure it works for you too.

Also, as with influencers, it's worth reading the ASA and CMA rules, but it's also worth making sure your ambassador is fully aware of the rules and adheres to them. Transparency is really important not just legally but also in terms of helping your ambassador to grow a personal brand with a loyal fan base.

Sponsorship

Remember the Venn diagram I mentioned before? We're now entering the third and final circle – sponsorship. This is generally the one that will cost you the most.

As I said at the start of the brand ambassador section, you're going to see overlaps here and that's fine, people can be all three things to you, but sponsorship can also be slightly different.

Sponsorship, as mentioned at the start of this chapter, is generally connected to a skill and often a sport related one. I'm not massively sporty but even I can't miss the tick that appears on the hats of some golfers, the heavily branded formula one cars and their drivers, the writing on the shirts of footballers, the names on the saddlecloths of eventers and their horses. They are usually sponsors. People who have invested in said sports person and helped them on their journey. In some cases, they may have paid actual money for that 10cm square space in prime permission.

Generally, sponsorship is the exchange of money for some form of advertising. It might be that a product is also exchanged as part of the deal, but it doesn't have to be. Company X who makes bottled water might want to raise their profile in a particular market so they could decide to sponsor an athlete in said market by giving them money for the promotion that association brings. They might do more, but that might be it.

Of course, sponsorship doesn't end at space on people's chests, not at all, most things can be sponsored. Events are a key one. As per the sponsorship of athletes, this is often done through the exchange of money for space and promotional opportunities connected to said event. The brand doesn't have to have anything beyond that level of interest in the actual event. Think of the names you see on hoardings of football stadiums, title sponsors of events, and so on. These brands will have some reason behind the support – maybe the people who go are their target market and they want to get in front of them – but unlike with ambassadorship, the personal connection doesn't really need to be there, it's a lot more transactional.

Sponsorship on its own is probably not something you're that excited about if you're reading a book about promoting your business for next to nothing. But it's worth keeping in mind as sometimes opportunities come along that have the potential to deliver an incredible return on investment (ROI) and I don't want you to have your blinkers on here and miss something really good, OK? Being able to identify something as good (even if you're currently lacking funds), seeing how things work and observing the benefits of that sponsorship can provide a brilliant learning platform. And also help to inform you if you'd like to sponsor something specific in the future.

As with brand ambassadorships, the contract/agreement and legal side is on you here as I'm not a solicitor. Generally, I would say contracts are far more common in sponsorship circles vs. brand ambassadorships but I would urge you to seek the correct advice on this, especially if money is changing hands, to make sure you're covered.

But what if I AM the influencer, want to be a brand ambassador or want to be sponsored?

The above should help you work out what you're prepared to do and what you might be able to gain from the support you might receive. You might get the seed of an idea about how to work with a brand you adore. You might start to think of ways you could promote the things you love. You might research contracts and agreements. You might start speaking to people in the same space as you to find out what pitfalls they have come up against to help you prevent falling down in the same place. And it can be really useful to see things from the other side of the fence. If you want to work with brands in any of these roles, the point is you're meant to be helping them achieve their objectives and having this in mind will help that.

ROI?

ROI/Return On Investment, or a posh way of saying 'is it worth it?'. This is something you need to consider when you work with someone on any level. The actual returns aren't always in the most obvious way, or at least not to start with.

The most obvious ROI you may see is sales. So, ambassador X wears one of your products or talks about it on their social media or blog and as if by magic you get the sales. This can absolutely happen with the right type of engaged following. I would say though, if this is what you're looking for, make it easy to track what an ambassador is delivering for you. You can do this through unique URLs to specific areas on your website, or people can use a code and get something like a percentage off or free postage. If you move into affiliate schemes where the 'promoter' (whether ambassador or fan) gets a percentage of each sale as a kick back with no additional cost to the purchaser, you'll need to up your game here and make sure you're on it. This isn't to scare you off at all, and there are lots of systems that allow the integration of affiliate schemes into your website to do this.

The great thing about this really obvious way is that you can see exactly how much revenue the ambassador or influencer has brought in. Well, kind of. If the customer uses the code or the link. Or if it's the result of one post that has driven an 'I MUST have this!' reaction. Sometimes purchasing decisions can be a slower burn, so it's worth being aware of this and not basing everything on this one measurable. Another thing I've noticed recently with bigger influencers in particular, is that they often explain how affiliate links work and that the customers won't pay a penny extra if they use the link. They also explain how someone can get that product without the affiliate element. Just in case. So, in this case you wouldn't necessarily know, as a brand, where that lead came from.

Adding value

Oh yes. While direct sales can be a great indicator, the right ambassador or sponsored person can add massive value to your brand in other ways. Maybe they help you create a new product, that you design using their unique experience/ struggles that will appeal to their audience? Maybe they produce stunning images that you are also able to use on your social media, blog posts and even adverts? Maybe they write beautifully and can create stunning blogs for you that help to promote a collection or concept or idea or season? Maybe they're amazing in front of the camera and can record how-to videos for you? Maybe they'll model for your next big photoshoot?

While these things might not directly add to your bottom line, think about it,

If they're helping you design a product that they can document, try and test and then market to their audience, that could be huge for you, quite a lot of fun, and a brilliant PR story too. Products with stories are fascinating and rather than 'well, people like it in blue so we made it in pink', having a really interesting story about its creation will sell and captivate people. More than this, just think of the content that can be gathered during the product's creation – amazing!

Photography does have a cost, as anyone who's ever hired a photographer will know. These costs are generally and usually absolutely worth it as quality imagery sells products, specifically online. The only reason I'm saying generally and usually is that I don't want you thinking that all photographers are worth their money. They aren't. Like every other professional you decide to work with, you have to do your research. The right photographer who gets your brand and has the skill to capture it (whether product or service) is worth their weight in gold. Many influencers have developed their own photography skills (because they need to due to the volume of content they put out there or they have befriended their own photographer and they have an arrangement or ongoing collaboration going on with them). If you can tap into any of the above, whether you share their amazing content as a repost/ share on your socials or you have specific shots for you, this can actually add up to quite a big saving.

Writing

Not all influencers are bloggers, some have created their business around social media and, if you decide that you're working with social media influencers only, this bit might not apply to you. However, if you're working with bloggers in the most traditional sense, by which I mean people who have grown their following and 'fame' through the words they write, this is for you. Some people have moved away from the idea of bloggers and blogs having value, but I believe they're wrong. I love reading a good blog and I enjoy writing them too, you know, when I'm not writing a book. Blogs can tick lots of boxes. Examples are:

- they don't have a word limit like many of the social media platforms, meaning you can get into detail about whatever you like
- you can choose the layout, so rather than relying on the design of a platform you use, you can promote your words in a way that feels on brand to you
- you can link to products on your website (as relevant) to ease the buying process
- you can encourage social sharing
- you can repurpose the heck out of it by chopping it up into smaller caption style bits, quotes for graphics and more
- blogs can have huge SEO benefits to help your site rank up there on Google, this does depend on a variety of factors but if you get the right keywords, etc, it can tick away in the background delivering leads straight to your website without it costing you a penny.

Writing blogs does take time. If you're also the head of finance, head of sales, pot washer and tea maker, you're likely to find that content marketing and specifically blog writing gets pushed to the bottom of your list. Don't feel bad about this, you're not alone. I think marketing tasks often get downgraded as they're not seen as essential. They are if you want to run your business well and grow, but no one is screaming at you in the short term if you don't post consistently on social media, or don't write your blog, are they?

You can outsource blog writing and there are many people who will do this for you. There are lots of content creators out there in the world, and if you're struggling you can look at places like Fiverr and People Per Hour. Depending on your product or service, or the tone you use in your content, you might find this quite tricky. However, if you have someone who gets your company, understands the product/service you sell and writes beautifully, you're golden, and you might find that your ambassador or sponsored person might do this for you. Another thing to try is transcription. I've tried a few different services over the years. Some are free, some you pay for the software, and some you pay per minute of the transcription. Some have been good. Some have been awful. Some I have assumed that the software has been thinking of something else at the time. But now I use a paid for version to transcribe some of my podcasts to help with SEO too.

Video

With video, having someone who you can work with can be a real life saver, especially if you're not that confident in front of the camera. I'm very pro business owners getting in front of the camera themselves but also appreciate that for some this feels like a herculean effort. If this is you and you have an ambassador who is game, see if they will record videos either with you or for you. Videos about the brand and products might work well as a dual effort, but equally you might find that they're up for doing a how to style video that works well with it being a solo for them. There's no doubt that video is huge and getting bigger and more influential all the time, and by not getting involved you're missing out. Don't do that. Find a way to make it work. You also have the additional benefit that the influencer/sponsored person might/should (please ask them!) share the video with their audience too.

Photoshoots

Obviously one option is to hire and pay for models. Again, I'm not technically against this if you find the right people, but with a growing push towards more relatable models, you could win here too. I know the phrase is 'real people' but I'm not entirely sold on this terminology, as models are, in fact, real people too. I do think it's correct to say, though, that not all models fit all businesses. If your ambassador or sponsored person is a genuine supporter of your business, maybe they were even a customer, they're more likely to resonate with your audience. What they might lack in posing credentials they're likely to make up for in lots of other ways. If you hire a good photographer, they should be able to help with the posing!

As I've mentioned, I've done a lot of work in the equestrian industry, and this is a place I've seen using the wrong models have pretty unexpected repercussions. Often, horse riders are muscly – not like The Rock, but they're used to moving hay, bedding and feed around, and then trying to get half a tonne of animal to cooperate. Now, clothing that's designed for equestrians is usually made with this in mind, so if you have a fashion model who is perhaps not that muscley (I mean why would they be if they're not moving hay and horses about!?) the clothes won't look right. Put the model in different clothing and they'd nail it, but sometimes for specific industries and products it doesn't work.

Another thing that's very evident with equestrian is the way non-horsey people are around horses. Horse riders spend their riding lives trying to perfect their position (the way they sit on the horse) to make them as effective as possible. One thing is how they hold their reins. You always have your thumbs on top and your little finger the opposite side of the rein to the rest of your hand. You also always strive to have your heels down. Now imagine you, as a diehard equestrian fan, saw an image of a 'rider' on a horse with their heels up high and hands like they were pushing a shopping trolley? If you're not horsey you might think 'so?' but think about something you're really passionate about. Maybe you're a car enthusiast and someone modelling holds a tool upside down? Maybe you're a climber and you see someone's harness is done up incorrectly in an image? See where I'm going with this? So, by using people who get it, you eliminate or reduce these issues.

Why start small?

You don't have to do this, but I can't think of a time that I have said to a client or anyone I'm advising 'yeah, throw all the stuff at them, it should work!'. I'm tight. I'm cautious. And I also know that people aren't always what they seem and I am damned if I'm risking 'all the stuff' on one person to start with!

If you start small, you can test a theory and a person with no real risk to you. Yes, all products have a value, and all time does, but one product or service session vs. a load is much easier to swallow if it doesn't work out. This idea also allows you to give more people the chance at once. And you know what? If everyone does well you've absolutely done a slam-dunk there and should pat yourself on the back!

Also, explain this to the person you want to work with. I'm pro being open and honest as much as you can and saying 'I'd love to work with you but I would like to try something with this product first' is a great response. If that doesn't work for them, that's fine too, they weren't for you. If they're game then crack on and see what happens. See what they do with what you've given them and start thinking about how this could help with other things you do. It's exciting.

The other very obvious benefit is that if that influencer isn't quite for you, it's much easier to leave on good terms and you don't have to start demanding the product/s back because the value you've 'invested' through product is so great that you can't afford to let it go. As I said above, even with all the checks, you won't get it right all the time. Sometimes people's situations can change too – as in things outside your or their control can mess up amazing plans. But if you haven't given them everything, you can wish them well and move on.

Do you need control?

As someone who's a control freak, I get that you might be struggling with the influencer conundrum. What if they say the wrong thing? What if the image isn't of your usual standard or style? You know what, if you want to work with influencers you're going to need to chill out about this.

When you choose to work with an influencer, brand ambassador or sponsored person, you likely chose them, amongst other reasons, for how they 'were' online and how they engaged with their audience – am I right? If this is the case, there's little point in you micromanaging every single thing they do. Not only could you alienate their following and pee them off, you're adding to your workload, which is not really the point.

Of course, I'm not saying don't keep the lines of communication open, and I'm not saying don't be helpful. If they want to know the technical details about something or the RRP, don't say 'well, what do you think?' but I would advise against micromanaging at every level.

If you do want to really keep a very tight rein on your influencer, you're cruising toward ad territory. This isn't an issue but be prepared that with control usually comes cost. If you want your person to post a specific number of times in a certain time frame and you want approval over copy and/or images, that's an ad and you should pay for that because it's likely to take the influencer more time to create and post that content. If you're working with someone short term vs. long term, this might have an impact on the level of control you feel is needed. Don't for a second think I'm saying ads with influencers are a bad idea. There's a place for everything. But just be aware of what you're doing and why you started down this road.

There are rules

When you work with influencers there are rules you need to be aware of. The ASA (Advertising Standards Agency) and CMA (Competition & Markets Authority) have guidelines that help to explain this to both influencers and businesses. It's all about transparency and how to label content, I know I've mentioned this before but it's important.

8. Websites

Ah... websites. Your little online home. The corner of the worldwide web that is your very special place to call your own. As you turned the page, I'm wondering if you're thinking 'well, I don't need one of those, I have social media', and if you did, read on my friend. And if you didn't, read on too. It's good.

Do I need a website?

Short answer – yes. Long answer – yesssssss. In all seriousness, I get a sinking feeling when people say that they don't. I'll tell you why. Facebook is INCREDIBLE. Instagram is AMAZING. But unless you're Mark Zuckerberg and his team, you don't really have any control over either of them. I'm sorry but it's true. If both vanished tomorrow, would you have a business or a brand? I'm writing this at a time when both platforms have had significant wobbles not all that long ago. The wobbles were short lived, but everything always comes into focus very quickly and as someone who does a lot of work on social media, it always makes me feel more than a little sick. But I also know that all of the businesses I work with would be OK if neither platform ever came back online again. Yes, they'd have to evolve and adapt their marketing, but they could still trade and still contact their customers, which is kind of key if you want to stay in business, isn't it?

I feel like if you weren't convinced to start with, you might still be thinking 'yeah, yeah, you're just scaremongering'. Trust me, I'm not. I don't believe that Facebook or Instagram will vanish tomorrow (I mean, if they do, a fair amount of this book is irrelevant so I'm hoping they don't), but I believe that things will change inside the platforms, because they do all the time. When new updates are released, you'll see ALL the posts about the algorithm screwing people over. In my Small & Supercharged™ Facebook Group, social media and reach are very regular recurring themes. What if the next update hurts your reach even more and a teeny weeny percentage of people see your posts? It could really hurt your business.

Of course, with your website, Google definitely plays a big part in the success of your website from a rankings point of view, but people can still find you through typing in your website address if they want to buy from you.

Not all that long ago, websites were expensive to create. By that I mean ALL websites were expensive. You can still pay a huge amount for a website now, but chances are it'll be packed with features that make it earn its money. Nowadays you can get yourself a website for... wait for it... nothing.

How much do websites cost?

I'm sure you've seen the ads on the TV that promise you a fully functioning website for free. Well it's a thing. Platforms like Wix allow you get yourself a website for free, but there are other options too. I use WordPress for my website and although my website does cost me money (I'll explain why in a mo), you can get yourself a WordPress website for free too.

When you look at your website and its costs, there are a few things to consider. Free options generally have something in your website address that links to the free provider. So, if there's a 'wordpress' in the URL, the chances are that that's being hosted for free by WordPress. If you buy your own domain name and want that to be used, you'll pay for this, whether you pay WordPress or another hosting company. But more on that later!

The template or design is another angle that you need to consider. There are LOADS of free templates out there that you can customise at will. And more than just being loads, there are lots and lots of really smart templates. Free doesn't mean rubbish here as there's a huge amount of customisation available on most of these themes that can allow you to elevate your site and make it look really slick.

My website is built on a paid theme/template. Both the free and paid for theme options are great for those on a budget. If you're on a teeny tiny budget, invest your time in looking at the free themes and seeing which will work best for you. Look at sites you really like and see if you can find out what theme they are running – you'll be surprised how many are using free ones! There's actually a website that detects the themes of people's sites and tells you what WordPress theme someone is running. That is, if they're using a WordPress theme!

As I said, I use WordPress, and with this comes the ability to add plugins which are little bits of software than can make your website do other things. Ecommerce plugins are available as are 'pop ups' (ones that encourage newsletter signs ups and more) and so many more, so, again, don't be put off if the theme you find isn't ecommerce. You might find a relevant plugin fixes that with ease.

And of course, there is the third option. A full-on customised build. Again, I'm not against this – I'm not against anything that is a good use of your funds, but you could be looking to spend a significant amount if you don't use any kind of pre-existing framework and you have to use the services of a designer. If you're a big ecommerce brand, then I completely see why you'd want to have a completely bespoke website. The online space is really competitive and having something that gives the perfect, on brand experience to your customers and prospects can be an incredibly good use of funds, especially if this means people are wowed and spend their hard earned money with you. But just be aware that, especially if you're looking to do this on a shoestring, this might not be the best route. Or more precisely it might not be the best route to start. But start you must. You can get a whizzy, bangy, all singing, all dancing website when you have some money to invest in it. By then you'll probably have a much clearer idea of what you want, because your freebie theme will have taught you more than you can imagine.

Regardless of which option you pick, you don't have to go it alone. You can pay a web developer to help you customise a free theme, whether you pay for additional hosting or not. There are also amazing tutorials all over the place that will help you on your way.

How to find what platform to use

I've mentioned Wix and WordPress above, but there are more than that. Other popular platforms include Squarespace, Shopify, Magento... the list is huge and I'm not here to tell you which to go for (sorry). I use WordPress myself, because I kind of fell into it and I like it so I haven't changed since. But then my website isn't particularly 'clever'. I sell my courses on a different platform called Thinkific (obviously I link from the website, but you know what I mean), and my membership group works via a website and Facebook group and a PayPal recurring payment link.

If you sell products in a serious way, you're going to want a website that makes the shopping experience really easy and this can vary hugely depending on your products and what your customers are like. If you're wondering where to start when it comes to what platform to use, I have some tips.

1. Ask. Seriously. If you're part of any Facebook groups, ask people what they're using for their website, what they think of it, and then go and have a look at their website. You might HATE it and the way it works or you might love it. You'll probably discover lots you didn't expect to find out by simply asking what people love about the platform they use and some of these might be game changers for you.

2. Research. And then ask! Think about the websites you really love using and then see what platform they're built on. If you scroll down to the bottom of the homepage, many sites show what they're running on. Some say, 'Powered by Shopify', mine even tells you the theme and the platform if you scroll down to the bottom. If you can't find out from their website, you could always drop them an email if you really love it. They might not reply but you never know your luck!

3. Explore. Some platforms will let you have free trials or see demos in action. Do the legwork and have a play with some you're interested in. You might find you HATE the Content Management System (CMS) that runs it, or you might find that platform edges ahead because the layout of the backend feels more intuitive to you.

Ray Gillespie has worked on websites for all different types of business and shares some wisdom on how to pick the right platform for you.

'There are literally millions of CMS to choose from, so how do you know what is right for you? Broadly speaking, there are two kinds of CMS solution available: hosted, and self-hosted. A hosted solution is where the CMS provider takes care of all the hosting for you, whereas a self-hosted solution allows you to host the website yourself or, more commonly, pay a web host/developer to host it for you. There are pros and cons to each, and it's important to work out which is right for you.

'Hosted solutions are great because they are simple to set up, and they usually provide a tiered-pricing model that lets you select a monthly price based on the features you require. However, this can also work against you as, especially when you are starting out online, it's not always clear what features you will end up needing, and you may find yourself spending more than you initially expected. You don't normally pay a specific hosting cost, as this is included in your monthly charges.

'Some of the top hosted CMS include:

- WordPress
- Shopify
- Squarespace
- Wix.

'Self-hosted solutions work differently and are generally provided free of charge for you or your web host to install on your own server or hosting space. While they are free to install and run, there may be some costs for 3rd party add-ons or plugins, and you will need to pay for an on-going hosting cost. However, you will usually find that self-hosted solutions give you the full range of CMS features without any extra cost, and it's often cheaper in the long-run to use a self-hosted solution, especially if you plan on expanding your web presence in the future.

'Some of the top self-hosted CMS include:

- WordPress
- Drupal
- TYPO3
- Magento.

'You may notice that WordPress is included in both lists – this is because WordPress is available in two versions: WordPress.com and WordPress.org. They are essentially identical, other than WordPress.com is a hosted solution and WordPress.org is a self-hosted solution.

'When choosing your CMS, it's important to consider whether you want to use a hosted or self-hosted solution, but don't let your preference restrict you – if you find a CMS that's perfect for your requirements and can afford the on-going costs, it's probably the right solution, regardless of whether it's hosted or self-hosted.

'Right now, the most popular CMS in the world is WordPress, and that's for good reason – it's well-supported, easy to use, with a massive range of themes and plugins available. Even though WordPress was originally a blogging platform, it has expanded to the point where it's the biggest website platform in the world, and is used for ecommerce websites, booking platforms and a multitude of other types of website. However, it can be a bit trickier to set up initially, especially compared to some of the simpler hosted solutions like Wix or Squarespace. If you're confident enough to have a go, WordPress is probably the best place to start for most websites.'

Web hosting

A lot of people are a bit confused by hosting and I get that, but I promise you it's actually really easy to understand, it's just the space where your website lives on the internet. Simple as that. Now, as you will no doubt want all your hard work to have a home, you're going to need hosting, but there are a few different options.

Free or paid for?

Like with domains, themes and everything else, there are free, cheap and more expensive options.

'To some extent you get what you pay for with hosting,' says Ray Gillespie, 'but it's important to consider the features that each hosting provider offers. For example, most websites require an SSL certificate to be installed, and some providers offer this at no cost while others make a separate charge for it. Equally, most hosting packages have some form of email provision, but you may find that you are given very small mailboxes (1GB or less), whereas other providers provide larger mailboxes (10GB+) included in the monthly cost. The age of the hosting platform will also have a massive influence on the cost vs. features offering, as newer platforms generally include a lot more for the money, so where possible look out for newer features such as SSD (solid state drive) storage.'

The good thing is that you can change between these options if you need to. Obviously if you go down from managed to paid, you'll lose support and maybe some other elements too, but you don't have to make a decision now and live with it forever. And more than that, if you want to switch between providers that's actually really easy to do. I've done this before and my website had no noticeable downtime so, again, don't worry about making a decision that might not serve you in a few years' time, you can change!

If you're looking at hosting and you're in the paid for/managed area of thinking, then I have some points to think on and ask your shortlist about. This is not a complete list but these are the things that matter to me specifically when I'm thinking of where my website lives online. If you have a big ecommerce site, you might have different questions, add them to your list and don't feel stupid about asking any questions. I always think that the reason you're working with someone is because they have better knowledge or more skill in an area than you do, so they should know more than you. With this in mind, they should be happy to answer your questions.

And something else about asking questions? Listen and look at how they respond. This goes for all services and products actually, but I've found it really useful here. I don't mind people being direct and to the point but if someone either a) treats me like an idiot b) throws a load of jargon at me and c) really couldn't care less at the stage when they're trying to woo me, we won't be working together. I have a thing about being treated like an idiot by people who want money from me. They don't align. I also have a real thing when people throw a load of jargon at me as it can mean they don't really understand the subject as well as they are suggesting – with true pros I have never had this issue. And point c really goes without saying doesn't it? If someone who should be trying to woo you is showing they don't care, you're screwed when they actually have your money. So, as you ask these questions, don't just listen to the answer, listen for all the other things!

Some hosting questions.

1. What packages do you offer and what would my website need? They'll probably need an idea of the size of your website for this answer BUT if you explain what's on your website they will probably have an idea too.
2. What kind of service to do you offer? Are they available 24/7 if there's an issue?
3. What's the uptime? As in, as a percentage, how much time do their websites stay up and fully functioning?
4. Do you do email hosting too? Website and email hosting aren't necessarily the same – some companies run these as two different things. You might also host your emails through another service.
5. How much space will I have for emails? If you do opt for email hosting too, ask how much space you're allocated.
6. How much will it cost? I mean, obvious really!
7. How are payments collected? Monthly/yearly, how?
8. Will you help me move my website/get set up? Managed solutions usually do, if you're just paying for hosting you may have to do the legwork.

Domains

I'm not proud to admit it, but I do have a bit of a thing about domain names. Some people collect stamps and if I let myself, I can collect domain names. But luckily they aren't (usually) crazy expensive for most of us, so it's not up there on the problem list.

Just so we're all on the same page, your domain is your website address. Mine is rheafreemanpr.co.uk, but I also own rheafreeman.co.uk, rheafreeman.com and about a million others. If you want to get started with your own online home, I would strongly suggest you invest in your own domain. You don't actually need to do this to get your own spot on the worldwide web, but I think having your own instantly makes you seem a whole lot more legit.

Don't misunderstand me here, to have your own blog or website, you will need a domain assigned to this, but if you opt for the free website, free hosting option, those names often have the brand woven in. But it's free, so it's your choice.

The very good news is that most domains aren't expensive. I say most, because a little search on Google revealed that the most expensive domain name ever, according to GoDaddy, was valued at a whopping $872 million. It was cars.com. Actually, if you have a few moments to kill, it's quite a fun list. Cars.com is in at number one, and carinsurance.com is very high on the list.

For most of us with brand names longer than one word, we don't have to sell possessions to afford our domain/s. If you have a look at websites like Fasthosts, Easyspace, for example, you get a better idea. To prove the point, I went for buildingyourbrandonashoestring and the .co.uk price was £10 for two years from one website. You can also opt for .com, .uk, .net, there's a load, and usually the less common endings are cheaper.

As for which to buy, don't buy them all because it will cost you a fortune, even for a really random name. However, in my own experience, I tend to go for .co.uk and .com. If one of these is gone, I wouldn't buy the other as I wouldn't want whatever I was doing to get confused with someone else, but that choice is yours. It might mean that you add another word to your website address or add a dash, just to make sure that it's really easy for people to find you and not get your brand confused with a brand of a similar name, which wouldn't be good.

If you're thinking 'but I only want one website?!' don't fear, having multiple website addresses doesn't mean you need multiple websites. You just need to make sure all your connected domains point to the one place you want people to come to. I have, as I said, a few pointing to my website, six in fact at the time of writing this. I know, I said I had an issue.

Buying domains is super easy and getting them pointing in the right direction isn't that hard. There are plenty of how-tos online if you're managing your own hosting, or you can call on your web hosts if you have a more comprehensive package to help you.

You don't have to buy your own domain, it's completely up to you. Personally, I think having your own domain, for both website and email, adds another layer of professionalism to your brand. You may disagree or you might not feel it's a priority at this moment. And that's absolutely fine. My priority in this chapter has been to promote the virtues of your own online space. How you get people there or its address is your call.

9. Search Engine Optimisation aka SEO

Search Engine Optimisation also known as SEO is one of those 'things' that is surrounded in mystery until it's explained and you think 'what, is that it?'. I'm not saying that HOW to get to the top of Google isn't challenging, far from it, but the idea behind SEO to me is pretty simple. It's to make your content as easy for Google (other search engines are available!) to index, to help people looking find whatever they need. As website owners, it's our job to do our best to help Google. Google is incredible, and it has to organise the world's content in a way that it can quickly match up a person's need or issue with the best place to get that answer.

Search engine friendly

I'm not an expert on SEO, so I've reached out to someone who is, to talk you through the first steps needed to make your content and your website more search engine friendly. It might seem like another thing you need to do, but if you're putting time and effort into creating content (and I mean things like blogs, vlogs, podcasts, etc), surely learning how to increase their chances of being found by the people who want and need them makes sense? That's what it's all about.

Tim Cameron-Kitchen is the MD of Exposure Ninja. Not only is Tim's business dedicated to helping people get their company more exposure online, but he's also co-authored a rather brilliant book (I have it on audiobook AND printed book!) called How To Get To The Top Of Google. I loved this book and, actually, the company's whole ethos because instead of trying to bury the reader is technobabble jargon, it was all very logical. As a side benefit, they also offer a FREE (and it really is free!) SEO review of your website. I've done this for my own business and have also paid for the upgraded version and have been very impressed by both. That's why I wanted Tim to help you with this.

'Whilst SEO can sometimes feel intimidating and confusing, I like to remind people that really you're just trying to make your website as useful as possible to potential customers. Most of the changes we SEOs make to websites are to make it easier for users to find their way around, and understand when they're in the right place.

'One of my favourite starting points to get you going is having a separate page on your website for each of your products or services is a great way to make sure that they have the best possible chance of ranking. By focussing each of your pages on a specific group of keywords related to a single product or service, you can give Google highly specialised content which is much more likely to rank than if you try to cover all of your services or products on a single page.

'One of the "quickest wins" when it comes to the more technical optimisation of a website is making sure that your target keywords are used in the Title for each page. This Page Title is a bit of code on each page which defines the text that shows up in the top browser tab, but is also used by Google as a signal to the keywords you think that page should rank for. In WordPress, your Page Title defaults to the name of the page. You can change this by using a plugin like All In One SEO Pack or Yoast.'

SEO doesn't just relate to your blog posts; it also relates to the other pages on your website, so keep it in mind whenever you write. But a word of caution here, and one I know that is very much in line with Tim's thinking, is that while you want to optimise your website for search engines, don't forget the next step. The people. In addition to getting people to your website, you also want people to stay on your website and consume the content they came to find. If it's written with spiders and computer wizardry in mind, it's going to lose its appeal to the reader. This will likely lead to a high bounce rate, which won't help you in Google's eyes, so your 'advantage' has been lost. Also keep away from any of these weird 'black hat' techniques. Please. If you do make any gains from this they will be short term. Don't try and cheat the system. You don't need to cheat it. You need to work with it.

Keywords and great writing

If you think 'meh, this sounds like something that's going to take forever and won't help me really', I'd like to introduce you to Marcus Sheridan. His business was in a very tricky position before he invested time into his SEO. He capitalised on the questions his customers and potential customers were asking him and created content around them. Due to the use of long tail keywords, great writing, dedication and so much else, the articles that Marcus wrote climbed up the Google rankings and drove more traffic to his website. And you know what that meant? More sales.

> 'Every minute, potential buyers of yours are asking questions online, just looking for someone who is willing to give them an honest, transparent answer to their question or search', says Marcus. 'But the sad thing is, most businesses aren't obsessed with what their

buyers are thinking, fearing, searching, and asking. They aren't willing to take the time to thoroughly answer those questions online. But the few that do truly obsess over what their customers and prospects are thinking, and then are willing to address those subjects honestly and transparently on their website, now they are the ones that will ultimately explode consumer trust, dramatically improve SEO, and directly affect their bottom line in the process.'

This is something that I have more than a passing interest in and, as someone looking to market your business for free, I would really advise you to take seriously too. SEO isn't an overnight solution to problems BUT has the ability to generate constant leads for years to come with no further effort from you if you tick all the boxes and I've actually had this experience myself.

Google Analytics

Through Google Analytics, I'm able to see what content is the most viewed. Google Analytics is free and provides an incredible amount of information if you explore it, but one of the most basic things it does is tell you how much traffic your website has and your most viewed content. In March 2018, I wrote an article about how to hide hashtags in Instagram Stories and I noticed that this blog kept bringing in traffic. It's old, so it's not content I'm regularly pushing on social media. Then I put my browser into Incognito mode and Googled 'how to hide hashtags in Instagram Stories' and then it all made sense. I was at the top. So, if you're looking for that and you type in this long tail keyword, you'll find my blog post about it.

Plugins

One of the things I use on my WordPress site to help my SEO is a plugin called Yoast. As you'd expect, I use the free version. I love this plugin because it analyses what I write and then provides hints that help me change the red or orange traffic light display, next to how my content has scored for SEO, to green. And that pleases me. In addition to looking at the copy you've written, your sentence/paragraph structure, keyword density and alt tags on your images, Yoast will also tell you if you need to add more headings, less headings, more words; it's very handy. It also produces a reading score that judges how easy your content is for the average human to read. I don't find this as useful as the traffic lights but I do like it. It can sometimes highlight things you've completely overlooked and it's definitely a useful reminder if you've forgotten to add a full stop to a paragraph.

10. Newsletters

Are newsletters dead? No, no they aren't. As I write this, one of my focuses is on growing my mailing list. It's not as much of a focus as it should be but I know the power it has. Even with a small list of the right people (that bit is key), you can support your business and that's what this is all about.

Does anyone even read newsletters?

Based on stats, yes they do. That is, if they care about what's inside the email. Think about your own inbox. If it's anything like mine, it receives a lot of emails each day, and many of these are newsletters. Do I read them all? Nope. But do I read the ones that interest me? You bet I do. Are you the same? See, I quite like having a gentle nudge when there's some great content out there that I might have missed on social media. We know that social media platforms only show our audiences a small percentage of our content initially and even then we are competing with a lot of people to get our message seen. Even in a busy inbox you're not competing with that many and more than that, at some point those people invited you in.

Open rates

Open rates and click through rates are key measurables when it comes to newsletters and there's no doubt that both of these figures aren't what they were. According to Campaign Monitor, the average open rate in 2020 was 18%[1] but this does depend on the industry. If you think this sounds low, have a look at the reach you get on your social media posts and then look at the engagement rate. Engagement rates on social media are worked out via action so a double tap on Instagram will do it. Is a double tap worth as much as someone actually opening an email and reading your words? I'm going to say no. But that's just me. So, while it might look low on paper, think about it a teeny bit more and you might change your mind!

One last point here is that if you grow your email list correctly (and that's not buying lists, it's about doing it properly and complying with GDPR as relevant), it's your list to market to. Something that shouldn't vanish overnight without any say from you. Even if you have just 20 people on your list when you start, you can contact those 20 people whenever you like (unless they unsubscribe). It puts the power back in your hands.

How much does it cost?

The beauty of starting to build your own list is that it costs you nothing. There are lots of different email marketing providers out there and many offer free packages for lower subscriber numbers. The one I use, Mailchimp, has a free option that allows you to grow your list to 2000 people, and send up to 10,000 emails a month FOR FREE. Well, at the time of writing this, that's the deal. I'm not saying that will remain the same forever, but just think of that. You could have 2,000 people who want to hear your views, promotions and product news and you could contact them up to five times a month (if you maxed out the whole list) for nothing. How good is that?

As with all free levels of paid for services, Mailchimp does have its limits. If you want more functionality or you exceed the magic 2,000, there's a monthly fee. I don't believe (at the time of writing this, again) that Mailchimp is the cheapest at certain levels, but if you're getting good open rates, click throughs and sales and you like the backend of the system and find it easy to use, it could well be worth its weight in gold.

Is it hard to set up?

It doesn't have to be. Most email service providers have robust how-to guides online, some even have videos that walk you through the process of getting yourself set up with an account and starting to build your audience.

I've used other platforms too, and the good thing is that inside the platforms, they help you design your newsletter, so don't let that put you off. Of course, if you have the money, then it might be worth getting a designer to help you really polish your email template, but I have to say that the templates inside these providers are pretty awesome and generally very intuitive. You can import your logo, change colours, some even have 'drag and drop editors' that allow you to put your text and image boxes where you want by just dragging them in place, making it really easy to customise an existing template or even create your own.

If you can't see exactly what you want or need some elements can be designed for you to integrate, Canva is pretty impressive. I feel like I should get this tattooed somewhere, but Canva really is amazing. Within Canva, there's even an email header that is the right size and ready for you to customise however you like. As usual, with Canva, there are templates you can pick (some are free, some paid for) or just get the right dimensions, put these into the custom dimension area when you're choosing your design and get started. You might find that in addition to the main header, you want to incorporate smaller graphics that point to specific areas on your website or social media. If this is the case, designing these inserts and using them over and over again can help you elevate the look of a newsletter as you get that brand consistency and keep driving that traffic back to your website.

Growing your list

This can feel overwhelming but I urge you to do this properly. There are lots of rules concerning email marketing and you need to be very aware of these, but you also need to be respectful of the people you're adding to your list.

It can be a bit deflating when you hear of people having mega email lists and you've got one person, who's actually your mum, on yours but everyone who has an email list worth having started at zero. So please just remember this. In growing your list one person at a time, in the correct way, you're on the right path to having a list that actually delivers something.

Quality vs quantity is as relevant for list building as it is for social media. I'm a bit obsessed with this, because I hate seeing people get deflated that they don't have a squillion followers. I get that. We all want big followings. But here's the thing – we want big followings of the right people. Like social media, having a squillion people who don't give a crap about you or your business receiving your email will likely do nothing for your brand. Actually, less than nothing. As mentioned above, larger lists incur larger fees when it comes to sending out emails and using the platforms. You'll be paying to, potentially, send out your email to people who couldn't care less. If the list is acquired in the wrong way, you're likely to see big unsubscribes too.

Then you have to think about why you're doing this. Because most businesses and personal brands don't need the squillions of people to have a really good, profitable business. But they do need people who care about what they're doing and are likely to convert into customers and true fans. Let's not get stressed about the number now, OK?

Sign ups

There are lots of basic ways to get people onto your list. A super easy one to get you started – just ask! Ask people who follow you on social media to sign up to your list and tell them WHY they should. Maybe they will be the first people to receive discounts and sales promotions? Your seasonal styling tips? Or your latest content when you send it out? Or maybe they'll receive offers from your favourite people. You're asking them for something that is theirs (their email address) that you want. More than that, you're asking them to give you a way to communicate with them whenever you fancy it. That's a big ask in today's world. You're adding to their workload, whether they read your email or not, so give them a reason to subscribe.

You can get a simple sign up form through your email marketing provider. In this case, you can usually customise the form in terms of colours, welcome message, opt ins and even what information you need, and then you have a link that will take people straight there. I also have a 'double opt in' on mine, which sends a message to the email address as soon as that address subscribes and then they're added to the list when they confirm the subscription. This process is all automated, I don't interfere with it at all.

This link will allow people to sign up to a particular list and that will help you develop specific audiences. Again, if you're using free email service you might find you have one audience as your option (as in, one list you can add people to) and that's fine too, but if you're paying you might be able to create different audiences. This might sound like a pain in the neck, but if you have a few different offerings or even a few different websites, you can make sure you know where everyone came from and what encouraged them to sign up. I have an overall audience and then I also have lists connected to the different freebies that are available on my website, so I know what is actually of interest to them.

So, now that we have the link and the idea, what do we do? We've asked people on social media, but again I'd urge you to ask more than once. Not day after day after day, but get it scheduled in to add a reminder to keep encouraging people to sign up by sharing the benefits of joining the list. Create a suite of different images that can be added to your social media along with the link to attract people and get posting.

Thinking of Facebook specifically, you can change the button under your header image to a 'sign up' button to drive people straight to your list and if you're so inclined, you can also incorporate a big arrow or call to action in your cover photo to get people there.

On Instagram, you can make the link to your list your link in bio or make a page on your website with links to all the places people might like. You can also add the link to your sign up form from Instagram Stories. Links on Stories used to be reserved for people with 10k+ followers, but that's no longer the case and you can add a link, whatever the size of your following.

Pop-ups might sound annoying but if you pick the right ones that don't nag people to the point that they never want to hear from you or see you again, these can work well. Some are timed to kick in when someone has been on your website for a specific amount of time, and there are other triggers too. Do your research as to what's available for your website. You might not want to add a pop up because you may hate them yourself but try and think slightly beyond your own hatred if you can; it might really help you.

The email signature, as in the bit at the bottom of each email you send, is another handy place to add a link to your newsletter sign up if you fancy, as is a confirmation email to a customer when they have purchased from you. The list of how you can just keep mentioning your email list is vast, and if you're feeling overwhelmed, just start.

Freebies

One way that has been tried and tested by many people is the freebie. This can be something as simple as a PDF that contains a short cut, how to guide, or something else, that people can have, for free, by signing up to your list. Well, I say that, you need to make sure that they don't have to be added to your list to receive your freebie. They should be able to sign up to receive the PDF but not be subscribed to your main list. They always need to be able to unsubscribe too, but I digress. Freebies have massive value.

I currently have three freebies on my website. I might even have more depending on when you read this, but all are useful to me and help to attract my target customers to different areas of my business. My newsletter subscribers get access to my freebies before they go on the website because that's one of the reasons that it's good to sign up to my mailing list – the content I put out, and that includes freebies. These freebies don't take me that long to make, actually very little time. The format of my current three is the same. It's a downloadable PDF that I have designed on Canva with five simple steps to help the person reading it to achieve a desired outcome easily. These aren't big documents, but they deliver results and they have helped me to connect with people in a really easy way. Not only am I helping them, but they get a feel for how I explain things, my style and more and I like that.

The freebies I create are delivered via automation. I am sure there are far more sophisticated methods but this one works at the most basic level. This stuff doesn't have to be complicated when you start. The more you add to what you do and the more functionality you add, the more complex the system becomes from the outside looking in. But again, this isn't something to fear. When you reach that point, you're likely to be far more confident with the system so it feels like a progression, and if you need help from a professional, you can always find someone who's really good at this kind of stuff and work with them. But the key is to just get started.

What am I going to say?!

Don't overthink this at the start because you might well talk yourself out of even getting started and you don't want to do this. You might think you're not interesting enough/don't have enough going on or that no one will care about what you have to say, but you're more than likely wrong there too – sorry!

Notes

1. https://www.campaignmonitor.com/resources/guides/email-marketing-benchmarks

11. Video

Video is the most incredible tool when it comes to helping you to grow your business, your reach, your following and your personal brand. As we've already explored, you need nothing more than your phone to get cracking.

Yes, you can absolutely work with professional videographers with oodles of kit, but to get started and in the true spirit of the shoestring approach, let's start at zero cost to you and work up. There are some incredible, mind boggling, stats out there around video. As more reports get created, and internet speeds improve, there's even more evidence to show that this really is the place to be,

Let's also spare a thought for the power of video and the part it has played during the Coronavirus pandemic too. Video, in so many forms, has helped businesses to grow and thrive in the most challenging of times, even when face to face selling wasn't allowed.

Even if the idea of getting yourself in front of the camera scares the living daylights out of you, please stick with this chapter. There are lots of ways that you can integrate video into your business's marketing mix and lots of reasons why you should.

Benefits

There are LOADS of benefits to video, over and above that of written copy and images. You might find that just a few of the following apply to you depending on your business, skillset or goals, but video can do all of the following.

1. Help increase your authority in a given field, or your 'expert status'. When we share our content, ideas and thoughts, if they're backed by some knowledge and theory, people will generally respect our opinion more. Why? There are lots of reasons why, and I'd ask you to think back on some of the people that you follow and learn from. What makes you trust them? To me, I love reading as much as the next person, but as we know, words can be edited and fine tuned to get the exact tone or feel. A first draft can be honed and edited to the point where the 'final' copy isn't a whole lot like the original and no one would know how many people were involved in that process. When you speak, even if you have a script, it's different. People can detect your knowledge on the subject and your confidence around it, but they can also get a real feel for you as a person and that can help to increase how relatable you are.

2. Help your customers. If you sell a product, you can use video to help your customers get the most out of it. This has got so many benefits. Showing people how to measure themselves for a product is likely to help reduce the amount of size related returns. Showing people how to check and test elements of their products might enable your customer to buy the right 'spare' for their product, thus reducing their time without it. Showing a product in use might encourage someone to buy something because they now believe they can work it themselves and can also see why they need it in their lives.

3. Allow people to get to know you. If you're developing a personal brand, beyond the 'expert' status, by getting on video you are allowing people to get to know you too. If you're more of a lifestyle brand and you're the face of it, people are actually buying into you. If you want them to buy into you and your name, you have to give them the opportunity to get to know you properly.

4. Share behind the scenes/exciting things/the making of. Video can allow you to story-tell around something you're really excited about, to share your unique experience with your following. If you're a product-based business, maybe you show the development or testing of a product. If you're a service provider, maybe you show a day in the life. If you're a blogger or influencer, maybe you show yourself getting ready for an event and your style tips. Or maybe even you take your fans along on the journey with you.

5. Day to day life. Whilst it's nice to see people with their glad rags on and brands showing us what they do best and their standout pieces, it's also nice to experience the day to day. This could be the people who make the business work each day, something that makes you smile each day, the offices you work in, or what your real life is like. If you have a bit of a poke around YouTube in particular, you'll see lots of vlogs around the day in a life theme, be these days out, days in or even what a family or child eats in a day. I find these weirdly addictive and I'm not the only one.

There are loads more ways that video can create massive value for your audience too. Think about the videos you like to watch, the people you follow and enjoy their content, the people you aspire to be more like and what kind of videos they produce. I'm not saying copy these people at all, but what I am saying is think about the content they put out and really analyse why they're doing it. Think about how it allows you to connect with them in a different way. Or what brands they can weave into their content that supports their bigger aim. Or how it makes you feel as a fan/purchaser of what they do.

Now think about how that could translate to you.

Practice makes perfect

I don't mind being the one to break this to you, because the whole point of this book is that I want to give you honest advice. OK? I mean this in the nicest possible way, but your first attempt will not be amazing. It might even be rubbish but you still must do it and get it out there.

I don't want you to read that and think 'well, I won't bother trying then!', but I want you to realise that everyone's first attempt isn't all that brilliant, especially when you look back 100 videos on. But it's an essential part of your journey with video.

When you film your first video, you'll probably be nervous – that's OK, actually, it would be odd if you weren't just a little bit apprehensive about doing something brand new for the first time. That is, again, normal and fine. To save you a bit of the pain that is so often experienced when people record video for the first time, I have some tips that will help massively. As you do more and more videos, these will become second nature and you'll also find other things that you do that make your videos better. But the key is to start. You can't improve on something you haven't done and all the best learning happens when you're actually doing the thing and finding your own way. So here are a few tips.

Have a plan

Some people plan their videos in the smallest detail as in, fully scripting them, and some don't. Some rehearse what they're going to say, and some have an idea and crack on. I'm in the latter camp. When I'm doing a video for my Mastermind membership group and it's our monthly masterclass, I'll jot down the key points I want to cover to make sure I don't miss anything, but it's far from scripted. To some people, this approach would make them come out in a rash, but to me, the over planning has the same result. If I try and script what I'm going to say, I lose connection with what I'm saying, my flow is broken, and I spend all my time staring at a piece of paper when in actual fact I want to connect with the person watching the video. To do that I need eye contact. Whatever way works for you, having a vague idea is good as it just reduces your stress levels.

Sound quality

Even though video is visual, sound quality has a huge bearing on a video's watch-ability and, therefore, the enjoyment and the value that the viewer gets from it. You don't need high tech microphones to deliver the kind of quality sound we're aiming at here. But you do need to make sure that you're giving your microphone – and that could be the integral one in your phone – the best chance of doing a good job. One of the enemies of quality sound is wind noise if you're outside, and background noise if you're inside. Wind noise can wreak havoc with sound (even if you don't think it's particularly windy) and render your carefully thought out words completely incomprehensible. Background noise can also be a big factor. Again, you might not even notice how loud your surroundings are but if your voice has to fight with a noisy setting or people talking you could well really struggle.

Background

You don't need an expensive backdrop but just have a quick look to make sure you don't have anything really random in the background that is at odds with your messaging. If you don't know what background would work for you, have a look at some videos you personally enjoy watching. You might find that a busier background works well for you and what you're trying to achieve, or you might want something completely plain. Gary Vaynerchuk has the most amazing, busy background behind his videos and I love all the paraphernalia that's on show that helps to tell a story about him and his passions. Conversely filming outside might be for you. Whatever you decide, own it, but just make sure there's not something there that is either sensitive (like a bank statement) or random (as I type this I have a load of plasterboard in my office which I wouldn't want in a video about social media skills!

Lighting

Getting your light right (or as right as you can!) can make a big difference. Just like with photography, natural light, if you can manage it, is an absolute godsend. You don't need expensive lights and I would suggest that if you're not sure how to use them, then artificial lights are best avoided. Some people use ring lights to help light their face, but I would honestly say, to start with at least, try and harness natural light. An overcast day can be ideal.

Testing, testing, 1, 2, 3

Always do a little test. This has saved me more times that I care to mention! Even when I'm filming Instagram Stories, I often do a little test to make sure the microphone is working (this is usually if I'm wearing headphones), but when I'm recording a video, particularly if I can't redo it easily, I test. Through doing this, even if you just say 'hello, hello, testing, testing' and watch it back, you can pick up on things like the sound and make sure you're happy before you launch into your video.

Add in a pause

Yep. Turn your phone/camera on, get yourself in position and then pause before you start and pause at the end. If you make a mistake that you want to re-record, pause and then go again. The pauses will be your friends when it comes to editing. Even if you're just trimming the start and end of your clip on your phone before you share it with the world, having that little bit of time can give you a much neater and more professional looking start and end. It might feel weird at the time but if you can do it you'll reap the rewards!

Keep it steady

I use a tripod for most of my videos but I also use a water bottle with a rubber band around it for some of the videos I shoot at my desk. My objective is to keep the phone steady and handsfree. Keeping the phone/camera steady will make it a lot more watchable and keeping it handsfree will be a lot more comfortable for you, and stop you having to twist into an odd position. Holding a phone steady for a minute is one thing; after five minutes it's more than a bit of a challenge! You can either invest in a tripod (and if you're planning to do lots of videos this is a good investment), but to start you can use a selection of books/water bottles and elastic bands or whatever works for you. It might not look like a Spielberg set up, but no one is going to see, so don't worry too much!

Slow down

When we get nervous we tend to speak faster. The more nervous we get, the faster we talk and fast talkers can be tricky to understand when you're not used to them. So just try and think about the speed you're speaking at when you're filming. Breathe and remember that the more you do the easier it'll become.

These tips will all help you with your videoing, but the best advice is to just start. In this case, practice makes perfect, and you'll be amazed at the differences you'll see even over a short amount of time.

You know I said your first attempt wouldn't be great? It might not be, but you're overtaking the people who won't put themselves out there and be a beginner.

Remember, what we think is rubbish; the reasons we dissect our performance – that hair that's out of place or the crease in our shirt – no one else will even notice. If they do, they won't care. They'll be listening to what you're saying and what you're doing, not whether your make up is perfectly applied. Putting yourself out there is a big deal, and with the people I work with, video often sets off more of their internal alarm bells than anything else but trust me when I say that it's worth it.

Landscape vs. portrait

Just to be clear and I'm sorry if this is teaching you how to suck eggs, I want to just touch on landscape vs. portrait. Landscape is when you film with the phone in a horizontal orientation, and portrait is when you film with the phone in a vertical orientation. Simple as that but worth thinking about.

In the olden days, before Instagram, I would have said that for any filming, landscape is the best, but now it's not that simple.

Both landscape and portrait videos will work on Facebook, Instagram, Instagram Stories and YouTube in one way or another. But just to keep us all on our toes, portrait videos LOOK the best on anything Instagram based and landscape videos look the best on the other two.

Instagram was developed as a mobile first platform, so it makes sense that this content looks better when the phone is orientated in the way that most of us use it, doesn't it? When you post portrait content on Instagram, even an image in your main feed, it takes up more space on your (and anyone else's screen), thus giving you a bigger splash on their feed and more scroll stopping potential. If you post a landscape video, a smaller video will be shown because it still needs to fit the phone's screen and with landscape the longest sides are top and bottom so there's much less to view.

If you put your portrait videos on YouTube or Facebook, they're likely to have black bars down the side. Is this a problem? It depends. The video will still work, it'll still function and your message will still be getting out to the world. But is it as perfect as it could be? Does it appear to be native to the platform? That's up to you. If you put a landscape video onto Facebook or YouTube, it fills the screen given to the video, which can make it look more appealing.

So how do you pick? In a perfect world, you'd film both, but this isn't a perfect world and we don't all have the time to film videos twice, so I'm not going to say that's an idea that's going to work for everyone. What I would suggest, though, is that you think of your most important platform at that moment. You should, of course, put your video in all the places you can to provide valuable content and insight to your fans and followers, but if your main focus is YouTube, for example, it makes sense to do everything you can to help it really shine on that platform.

Initially, landscape videos just didn't work on Instagram TV as it was, so the fact that they do now is a real blessing and allows you to use the same video in all the places you want.

Should I use the same video on all platforms and do I post natively or not?

This is a horses for courses thing too and there are different ways of looking at it.

If you REALLY want to grow your YouTube subscribers, let's say, then you might not want to post your video on all your platforms because you want them to head to a specific location. If this is the case, creating a little teaser (which might just be a small amount of the full video) on your social media platforms could well tick the native box too and give your content a bit of a bump. You could then use this teaser and in the caption (where possible) link to your YouTube video. Easy.

However, if your main objective is to get your content seen, then posting the same video on all your platforms, natively, is the best way to do this. By posting natively you're increasing your chances of engagement because the platforms are set up for this. One example of this would be Facebook's autoplay function that can kick in on native video (you know those videos that just start playing as you scroll?), which can make people stop scrolling in an instant. (I can't be the only one who's been sucked into a video about icing cakes, can I?) You can also add things like subtitles, natively inside Facebook which is a really good idea because stats say 85% of people use Facebook without sound. It's also really easy.

With Instagram, if you post natively to this platform, you can also share in your feed by moving the slider for that option, share up to Stories. If you use Stories for a short teaser, you could add a link to another destination using the link sticker, or you could suggest people go to your bio and pick up the link from there.

As for when, the general advice is not to post everything at the same moment on all your platforms but stagger it a little. It can serve as a reminder to people if they see it more than once at slightly different times. if you do post all of them at the same second your fans are likely to get a bombardment of notifications at the same time which does somewhat dilute what is going on.

Let's talk about kit

One of the 'blocks' that people have when it comes to video is kit, as in they don't have the 'right' kit, they don't have enough money to buy the right kit and they don't know how to use it.

Is that you? If it is, this won't be a block for you for much longer.

See, I'm not asking you to make the next blockbuster film. I'm asking you to make a video and all you need to do that is your phone.

Your phone might not deliver the highest quality video in the world, but we are not actually after that. We are aiming at a clear, easy to understand video that your fans and followers will get value from; that is all. If you follow the tips here you can achieve this easily. Just with your phone.

If you want to invest in kit, I'd say the next thing would perhaps be a microphone. But again, this doesn't have to be a costly one and you might actually find that using the one on your earphones will massively improve the quality of the sound on your video. If you have earphones with a microphone then try it out and do some testing with and without and see what sounds better. You can, of course, upgrade when it comes to microphones, even for your phone. I have a couple of different ones – I have a lapel microphone that plugs in and then clips onto a top. If I'm doing serious filming, I might use the lapel one and although I am sure the quality of my audio would be better if I used it more, I rarely remember so most of the time I stick with the phone's integral microphone. If I make sure background noise and wind noise are low/non-existent, it more than does the job.

I've mentioned stability being a big deal in filming, so if we're looking at kit and upgrades, a tripod is a good option. Again, I'm telling you this because I WANT you to love video and I want to support your quest to produce better and better videos, not because you NEED a tripod to get started. I can 'create' a tripod out of rubber bands, water bottles, pen pots and books if I need to, so you don't need to invest before you get started. Just start. If you want to upgrade your kit then a tripod is a good way to do that.

I'm no tripod expert (I own a few tripods, that's all) but there are a few things I have learnt that may help you. First of all, I'd go to an actual physical shop and have a look at some in real life. I like a bargain as much as the next person (maybe more) but with some tripods you can really feel the difference in the quality and the weight. I wanted something that was hardwearing, robust, easy to adjust and I wanted the panning movement (where you sweep side to side or up and down) to be smooth. I've filmed a few horse related videos in my time and you don't want a horse's trot to look jerky when it isn't. Trust me on this!

My tripod wasn't the cheapest but it wasn't the most expensive by any stretch of the imagination; I think it was £70ish and I'm SO pleased I paid that money. I have different holders for it that allow it to hold my phone OR my iPad Pro (the HUGE one) which I use to record the videos for my membership group and courses, and it's a game changer,

Another benefit of a tripod is if you have the space, you can leave it set up and make your own filming corner or area where you're happy with the background, the natural light is good and you're comfortable. Having a tripod set up here can massively reduce faffing and setting up time if you're going to film in the same place.

Lighting might be another purchase but be careful with this one. There are different lights available from soft boxes to ring lights and I think my general advice would be to use with caution. The idea of artificial light is a good one – who wouldn't want to make a dark room lighter for filming, but if you use the artificial light badly and it's leaving crazy shadows all over the place, it might not help you. The school of YouTube will help you understand way more about this, but if you're looking into artificial lighting, I would definitely spend a bit of time on Google to see what you might need, how that might work for you and learning how to set everything up correctly. Or else you'll have your shiny new lights, try them once and feel a bit disappointed with all the new shadows you've acquired.

Editing

One of the beauties of video is that if you mess up, you can simply go again and edit it out. Or just go again altogether. You might think that, again, you need really expensive, clever software to do this and years and years of experience, but to get started, you don't.

A way to reduce your editing stress is to not mess up. I know that sounds ridiculous but hear me out here. The more you do video the less you will make mistakes because your confidence will grow. So, if you're planning a three minute video and you make a mistake, you might find it's actually better to get to the end of the video (as a rehearsal almost) and then stop, restart, and go again because it's likely to take you longer than three minutes to edit it. So that's one idea.

If you want to just trim the beginning and end of the video quickly, your phone should allow you to do this without any further software. I have an iPhone and I can do this through the Camera Roll by just pressing edit. This means that if I do a video using my phone, as long as I've paused before I start talking and when I stop talking at the end, I'm all good.

Now, if you want to do more than this, you will probably need some additional software. Again, don't panic about this. With iPhones, iMovie is free and with Android/Windows devices there are a range of different editing options. However, I'm not going to get into the nitty gritty because I only do very basic editing on my phone and anything more complicated gets referred to my husband, Laurence, who does my video editing. However, all software is different so to try and give you some tips that work for everything, I'll hand you over to Laurence.

'You can choose to edit your own work or have a professional to do it for you, depending on your budget and skill level. On the one hand, a pro is likely to do a good job and free you up to do something else, but as this is a book about working on a shoestring, let's take a deeper dive in to doing it yourself. Coincidentally, even if you chose to have the work done professionally, the following tips will help them get the most out of your content.

'To ensure the finished video is as good as it can be, the filming conditions need to be as optimal as you can make them. Quality audio is a must, being aware of background noise is crucial, background, camera settings, and so on. If these aren't good, editing the video is a lot harder.

'Be prepared to edit, it does not have to be a one take perfect job from beginning to end. Having that as a goal will only make you panic when things go wrong and get you flustered. This will probably mean you make more mistakes moving forward. There is always a barking dog or ringing phone or parcel delivery just at the wrong time. Just remember it can be sorted, take a deep breath and when you are ready go back to the start of the last sentence and go again. Resist the temptation to carry on from the last word you said as this never edits well and will causes you a headache later. Also, leave gaps at the start and end of your recording, this will make it easier to edit and add the fades, effects or music you might want, I would recommend you count to five in your head before talking and at the end. Rhea still does not do this and it drives me mad!

'As for editing software, only 10 years ago editing software was limited and prohibitively expensive. Now you can get free apps with your smartphone or download them to your PC. iMovie, the free software you get with any current iPhone or Apple computer is more than capable of handling basic editing requirements and is all that most people will need. There are many free online videos to teach you how to get the most out of the software and it is worth taking some time to learn the basics. If you have a lot of video editing to do, I can highly recommend Apple's FinalCut Pro X. If you go for this, it will allow you to take your editing to another level but really is only necessary if you have outgrown the free software options.'

Making your video work really hard for you

When you've produced your video and uploaded it to YouTube, Instagram and maybe even Facebook too, make sure it really works its backside off for you because when you put that much time and energy into something, you need to make it pay.

One really simple hack is embedding your video into a blog. In most cases you can embed your YouTube video into your blog, meaning that when people view it, it adds to your YouTube views too. To add extra SEO benefits, you could blog about the videos and explain the concepts talked about inside it. You could even transcribe (or pay for a transcription service) that you could then link from your blog for people to download if they wanted. You can actually get things transcribed really cheaply online for something like 25p a minute at time of writing if you want to. Not only can this, again, help your SEO, but it makes it super easy to extract quotes from your video if you have all the words in front of you.

Why would you need to extract quotes? It can help you get more eyeballs on your video content, website and blog.

When we talk about the same thing over and over again, it's important to have variations. When we promote content on social media, not everyone sees our posts, granted, but there's likely to be some overlap when you consider the people who saw it the first time around are likely to be people who see more of your content because they have signalled, in some way (usually through engagement) that they're interested in it. So, if this is the case, you might want to switch up your messaging each time and attack it from a slightly different point of view to keep them entertained AND increase your chances of appealing to more people.

Let's say you've filmed a video of you making a cake, and your first push says something like 'This is my favourite cake ever – see how I make my Victoria Sandwich'. That's great for people who make Victoria Sandwiches, but in your transcription and in your video, you might talk about why you use sieved jam because of the pips, or a trick you use to make your buttercream extra light, or that it's an all in one method, or how you can do it in an hour, or some tips for decorating it, so you have your one video, but there's SO much value in it and it can be approached from so many different angles.

Now, the jam thing might not appeal to someone who doesn't care about the pips, but the fact you can have the cake completely done in an hour might. Or the fact your buttercream trick can solve an issue for a Delia wannabe. Also if the same piece of content is being served to the same person, you're still delivering value to them, each time they see it.

In addition to the variables, please, PLEASE don't let your amazing content get forgotten. Hands up, this isn't my strongest area, but I use a website called SmarterQueue that helps me with this. There are others like MeetEdgar too, and these recycle the content you ask it to and you can add variations as well. This means your evergreen 'how to make the best Victoria Sandwich' gets recycled as often as the system set up allows with no additional effort to you. When I say recycled, I mean promoted again.

This doesn't mean you can't wheel it out and promote it for village show season, or any random day connected to cake, or jam, or summer, but it means that it won't get forgotten and your work won't just be there for people to stumble across it via your SEO.

Going back to the blog idea, you might choose to write a different blog that would still allow you to promote your video and embed it again. Going back to cake, how about a blog about your top five jams, or best fruit for jams, or ways to use jam, an interview with the company who makes the jam you use, etc?

Chop it up

Don't think your video can only be played in its complete form all the time; there might be other ways that you can make it work for you. We talked about the teaser video leading to the full length video on YouTube, but you might also find that you can make smaller 'complete' videos using your 'big' video. This would work well on platforms like TikTok, Instagram Reels or YouTube Shorts. Going back to cake again (sorry), you could lift the section of your video when you show how to make the butter cream and run that as a standalone video. Maybe you add a voiceover and add a new intro and outro (and maybe you link the full video in your caption), but in doing that, you have a nifty little 'how-to' you can post where you like. You could lift the bit where you talk about benefits and downfalls of the all in one method as another standalone clip. Is there a hack to sieving jam to remove the pips?! I've no idea, but your lifted clip showing you do this might well reveal that there is.

This is one fictitious video about making a cake. What could YOU do with your brand, skills or products?

12. Podcasts

I love podcasts, not just to listen to them, but to produce too.

From a listening point of view, podcasts are free and if you choose well, you can learn absolutely masses while you're doing something else. I like to listen when I'm walking the dog, or driving, or if I'm doing something in the office that doesn't require that much brainpower – like tidying!

Flip that around – how much would you like to accompany people on their walks and on their car journeys without having to leave the comfort of your own office? That's why I started mine, the Small & Supercharged™ Podcast if you'd like to check it out.[1]

Podcasts are a brilliant way to let people get to know you and your expertise in a really low stress way. You won't know who's downloaded and listened to your podcast (unless they tell you) and this alone can make it a really appealing way for people to engage with you.

When you produce your own podcast, you can talk about whatever you want for as long as you like, upload this to your hosting platform and then it gets distributed to the world with no further effort from you. Like blogs, this content can be consumed immediately, a day after release or even years after release if the content stays live and you continue to add to your library and get discovered by people who might be interested in working with you in one form or another.

Podcasting equipment

If you decide a podcast would be a good way forward for you, your next question might be around kit. As with everything, there are many different ways to attack this situation and as with everything in this book I'm here to tell you that there's a budget way. In this case, the budget way might not be the best (although I have to say I have heard some amazing podcasts recorded with minimal kit) but what it will do is allow you to start. And as with everything, the first step is pretty blooming important.

The first thing you're going to need is a recording device. I use my MacBook Air to record all my podcasts and use free software QuickTime if I'm recording a solo show or I use Zoom (again, there's a free option here) if it's an interview as this allows recording on a voice or audio call through the computer. I don't have a PC but all you need is a pretty basic audio recording programme. And, although I use Zoom and QuickTime you don't have to. You can use whatever you like. The point here is just to show how easy it can be.

Another alternative that I haven't used myself (but have heard podcasts that have been recorded in this way) is just through the phone. I do record various different audio notes and ideas on my phone and I use the Voice Memos app, and on further investigation, it's very possible to record a podcast through this free app on your phone. Of course, there are some other more specific podcasting app alternatives that have more functionality inside the apps that would be worth exploring as you get into it, if the phone is going to be your friend for this.

Now you have two solid options to record the podcast on, we need to get a tiny bit more detailed. Not too much – this isn't a definitive guide to podcasting, but I want you to have enough information to think 'hell yes, I can do this!' if that is what you want to do.

Where to record

With a podcast, the only thing you have to worry about is the audio quality, so it needs to be as good as possible. There will be times when various things will screw you over and the audio isn't the quality you'd like, we all have that (and more than that, I've heard some chart topping podcasts with variable audio quality, so don't sweat it), but it needs to be as clear, crisp and clean as possible. We're going to touch on microphones next, but the environment is a big deal and even with a good microphone, if you're in the middle of a windy field you're going to struggle.

When you record, you want to make sure that there's silence or as close to silence in the background. No radio. No TV. Ideally no angry children or barking dogs, traffic noise, ringing phones, computer notifications or car alarms. Of course, if you have a child or a dog and you're in the same house you might have an issue if something causes upset or the postman arrives but do your very best. Your audience will thank you.

Also consider the room you're recording in. If you're in a big room with lots of hard surfaces and not a whole lot else, the audio is likely to be a bit more echoey than somewhere with soft furnishings around you. Equally, smaller spaces generally work better but from my experience the soft surroundings really change the game. The perfect excuse to invest in a few more cushions and throws, right? Or at least move all the best ones into your recording zone. A lot of high ranking podcasts are recorded in cupboards and closets!

Microphone

The microphone is important when you record, but before you think 'oh no, I don't have one' you do. Your computer will more than likely have an inbuilt microphone, and your phone will too. So, you have your basic level here. Now, as with the video advice, if you use your phone, try using your earphones and the microphone to see if that helps. Actually, you could use your earphones with your computer too (subject to the correct ports/adaptors). If you want to step it up, you can have bigger external microphones that connect via USB. There's at least a step beyond that too, but it does start to get expensive.

I'm at the USB microphone stage. But the thing I notice that makes a massive difference is the room I'm recording in. If I get them both right everything sounds SO much better.

The thing is you're not going to know what works for you until you try. I usually record my podcasts in my office, which has more hard surfaces than I thought and not all that many soft furnishings. The plus is that I'm less likely to get disturbed because it's away from the house. But the negative is that the sound can be a little echoey sometimes. So, I've now moved locations for recording to a much smaller but significantly more padded area. You don't need a lot of space to record a podcast. You just need to be able to fit yourself and whatever kit in there in comfort. That's all.

Editing

Most podcasts require some editing. Even if you're absolutely word perfect, most podcasts have some form of introduction (even if it's just a little jingle) and some kind of end too. If you're doing an interview, you'll probably need to add a vocal intro during the editing phase, but if you're doing a solo show you might not. The thing is, this isn't as hard as you may think.

My long-suffering husband, Laurence, edits my podcasts for me. I'm lucky that he's very good at this type of thing (and video editing too, actually), but I know many people who edit theirs themselves. Alternatively, you can hire editors. If you're not sure where to start, sites like People Per Hour could really help you or you can always send me a DM and I'll connect you to Laurence if he's got some capacity.

As per the recording software for video, some of these have inbuilt editing options that allow you to record, edit and upload on the same device, which can be really useful.

Hosting

Much like a website, your podcast needs to 'live' somewhere, so you will need to find somewhere to host it online and like websites, there are lots of different hosting options.

If you search 'Podcast hosting' you're likely to be greeted with a lot of options. They range from free to quite a lot of money and as with everything it depends on a number of factors.

I host my podcast through Libsyn and I pay to do so. The payment structure starts at just a few dollars a month but scales up depending on the amount of storage you need. With this host, that's the only 'thing' that links to the amount you're charged. I went with this host because Jenna Kutcher, the amazing lady who produces one of my favourite podcasts, The Goal Digger Podcast, recommended it on a podcast she recorded about podcasts (which is definitely worth a listen). With a chart topping podcast I thought that she would be a reliable source and she was right! She's currently featured, along with some other notable podcasters, on their login page too.

With Libsyn, when you upload (which is super easy), you get to add the title, description, cover image, etc, and you also get to select where you want the podcast to be published. Within the platform it's really easy to set up a variety of different places – or at least submit your podcast in the hope it will be accepted. When you have it all set up, you don't need to do it again, it'll just publish your podcast wherever you've asked it to.

Another really useful thing to do with this podcast is to embed the code generated from the hosting company in your website. This means that you can add that code to a blog, and people can listen through your website too. This might sound a little odd because a lot of people listen to podcasts through their phones, but people do also listen through the computer. The code is really easy to embed; it's genuinely a two second job, you just copy and paste it into your show notes. Simple.

Show notes

You may hear people on podcasts say, 'and if you look at the show notes….'. This might feel like another effort, but I think it's a must. The exact format these take and how they look is completely up to you, but I do think that they are really important in some format.

At one extreme, you can have the podcast transcribed fully and write show notes that go into a lot of detail around the podcast conversation and link to all connected sites you mention in the podcast.

In a perfect world, I think everyone would do this. Through writing detailed show notes you're also helping your podcast get the SEO benefits that a blog post would have and if it's a long blog that could be quite beneficial.

However, you might not fancy this, and that's OK too. At the very least, you could embed the code mentioned above into a blog post, write a really quick summary of why someone would tune in and listen, and maybe list all connected links below the 'player' you embed. This means that rather than reading out the full web address of a great resource (and we all know that some URLs would take you a while to read out and no one would remember where all the dashes and dots were), you can just say 'all linked in the show notes'. I know that I have listened to so many podcasts that say this and I've headed there when I've got back to the office to find out more.

Collaboration

Interviews can make great podcasts and with technology like Zoom, you don't have to be in the same country as your guest. In 2019, I recorded a podcast with the legendary Denise Duffield-Thomas author of Get Rich Lucky Bitch, Lucky Bitch and Chillpreneur. A lady I have admired for a long time if I'm honest. She lives in Australia, so without the kind of technology we have today, it just wouldn't have been possible. The only issue was the time difference and I think to date her podcast is the only one I've ever recorded at midnight. But it was worth every moment.

Of course, you don't need to interview people on the other side of the planet for your podcast, you could work with friends, brands you love, people you know your audience would get value from and people whose audience you'd like to know about you. Through collaborating on interviews, you can do all of this. You just need to make it work for you.

As with blogs, videos and even following people on social media, with podcasts listeners don't need to pick just one, they can have their whole device full of podcasts to listen to if they like, so don't fear collaborating with people who have their own podcasts. Don't fear collaborating with anyone in this way. It can be brilliant. And in my experience, it can give you the chance to chat to people you wouldn't normally be able to. Always think of what's in it for them just as with all collaborations, everyone should win when you work together.

Oh... and if you're thinking 'what if they say no?' well what if they do say no? If you invite them on, a clear benefit for them and also clear knowledge of them as a person, what have you got to lose? Seriously? In the first year of my podcast being in existence I interviewed Carrie Green (founder of the Female Entrepreneur Association) and Denise Duffield-Thomas amongst many other incredible people within my industry. These people said yes and I had THE BEST time interviewing them. So, who might say yes to you?

Repurpose

Longer form show notes (by which I mean the lengthier ones that are more than a quick summary and links) are a great way of making your precious podcast break a sweat for you. When you put the time and energy into creating something like a podcast, you want as many people as possible to hear it and you want to extract everything you can from this to do it.

So, one way to repurpose is to write detailed show notes, but you can also create additional blog content from what you've said. Maybe you could do a freebie download that highlights five key learning points from the podcast? Or how about a blog doing a deeper dive on one point you covered? Or maybe three things you've learnt from an interview with X about Y? You can then use this content as a standalone blog while still linking to the podcast at the bottom for people to find out more.

Quotes and snippets can be a great way to make a podcast work hard for you because we all know how much people enjoy quotes and facts, don't we? More than a straight up repurposing that you can then post on your social media as standalone content, having quotes pulled out and put onto attractive graphics can be a great way to promote the podcast too.

As a standalone, you could simply extract a really good quote or tip that you know people will love or is relatable/educational/inspiring and design it into something visually appealing using Canva (or other graphic design software). Get it right and this has the potential to be shared, saved, pinned and everything else across social media, helping to expand your reach.

But what if you added information relating to the podcast in the caption? This doesn't have to take away from the quote being standalone content too, far from it, the quote or tip pulled out should be strong enough to stand on its own, but where's the harm in adding a little context? And telling people where they can find out or hear more? No harm at all in my view, not if it's done well, of course.

Tell the world

And then you have to promote the podcast. If you have it all set up with your hosting company, the podcast will be automatically put onto the different platforms you ask and subscribers to that podcast will get it downloaded onto their device automatically, but please PLEASE promote it too. If it's taken you time to produce and you're using it as a promotional tool for your brand or business, you have to tell people about it!

Many of the repurposing ideas above can help you to promote your podcast too but being blatant is also a good call! I have a post that goes out every Wednesday morning on Instagram (at the time of writing – and on @rheafreemanpr) that talks about my podcast in the caption. I also share that post (I make it native and add links) on Facebook later that week. Then I create an Instagram Story around the podcast (both sharing the post up to Stories to talk about the podcast) and I also usually do a number of video Instagram Stories talking about the podcast and telling people how they can listen. Then I publish at least one quote around the podcast each week and then I ask people who listen to share it too.

Oh yes, I ask listeners to screenshot, share to Stories and tag me and a number of them do! Not everyone, but I'm eternally grateful to those who do as it's helping me spread the podcast to new people who might be interested. I also ask for reviews and ratings on the platforms people listen on.

And then, if it's an evergreen podcast, it gets added to my list to get up on SmarterQueue to be added and reshared at a later date.

That's just one podcast and I KNOW there's more you could do to repurpose it and make it go even further.

Notes

1. https://www.rheafreemanpr.co.uk/equestrian-country-business-podcast/

13. Public Speaking

Can public speaking actually help you promote yourself? OH MY GOD, YES. But is it scary as hell when you start? That would be a yes, again.

I'm going to tell you a bit about my own 'challenging' relationship with public speaking. I write this on better terms with it than I was a few years ago so rest assured that if you want to improve, you can and also be assured I have flipping miles to go to become the public speaker I want to be.

Generally, up until 2018, I shunned public speaking because I was rubbish at it. Or at least that's what I'd been telling myself for a very long time. Whether it started in school where I hated reading things out loud for fear of cocking it up, or looking back on it and being very close to vomiting at a press launch I'd organised, I don't know.

But whatever, these things sort of grew out of hand. Looking at it with a rational head on, I reckon most people aren't wild about reading stuff out in the classroom at school and make mistakes and I would also imagine that most people have felt real nerves when it came to a big event they had spent a lot of time planning, that they really wanted to go well. Right? But before I really addressed this and started to think about it, I just decided I was straight up rubbish at public speaking. Awful in fact. Then I had a moment and decided I was really done with feeling like that.

I did what any normal person would do – I applied to give a TEDx talk. I'm being sarcastic; these are not the actions of a normal human, but I did it anyway. I'd become more interested in TEDx since someone I was in a business group with on social media gave a talk. I loved her talk, the energy around it all, the organisation itself and became a bit hooked on TED and TEDx talks so I did the only thing I could and applied.

I think I applied for one or maybe even two before I got the green light and had a lovely email saying that they would love me to speak at TEDx Malvern. Then I realised that this meant I needed to actually deliver a talk in front on a room full of people and a video camera and that this would then be published on TED's YouTube channel. OH CRAP.

Not to be defeated by my own incompetence, I set to work. I was confident on the subject matter (if you go down this route to shake yourself out of a belief, please make sure you're good in this area, it's fundamental), but beyond that, it was new territory.

My first step (after the excitement to terror cycle that lasted maybe 10 minutes) was to buy a book. It was actually a bit of a game changer. It was a book by the head of TED – Chris Anderson, and it was all about public speaking, called TED Talks and it was SUPERB. If you're looking to improve your prowess on stage then please get a copy of this. It's brilliant and beautifully written. I read the book and felt a whole lot better about the situation. I wrote my talk again that was OK – it was all about how social media can unite rural communities and luckily I have an amazing client and friend who lives in New Zealand and she had a lady from a remote village in Norway who joined her online membership programme. Both of these connections were made via social media. As I say, without wanting to blow my own trumpet here, the subject wasn't the issue, I was excited to share a real life example and get people as enthused (well maybe not as enthused but, you know, remotely excited) about the good that social media can do. Because it gets a lot of stick for being the devil in disguise, doesn't it? Then I needed to do slides!

Now, I don't know about you but I have a love/hate relationship with them. Definitely on the hate side (but I imagine this is from seeing a few too many bad uses of slides in my time). When people use them in talks, I mostly zone out of anything that's coming out of their mouths and just read the slides so I knew mine couldn't be like that because if I was putting myself in that position and could well make a fool of myself, I needed people to be listening. Which sounds an odd thing to say. But it was and still is very much my belief I'm all in it seems! So, I sat down on a Friday afternoon to do the slides and I HATED every single template and design inside the two different software options I could pick. So, I did what anyone would do who was terrified they were going to make a tit of themselves and I designed them all myself from scratch on Canva before importing them all into the software. It sounds silly but having the slides exactly how I wanted made me feel better. Because when you do these things you want everything that can to be stacked in your favour.

I also decided to make a bit of a thing about what I was planning to wear. I did this for my second TEDx talk too. As I work with a number of incredible product based businesses, I was able to loan various bits including a jacket (with a dark background I felt I needed something lighter) and some amazing jewellery and that, again, helped. Because if you feel comfortable, you can do more. Or at least, it helped me. Part of me felt I should have rocked up in an amazing dress or skirt, but I don't usually wear either of these things, so I would have felt pretty uncomfortable and I felt I had enough to think about.

As the day got closer, I practiced my talk. Then wrote onto cards with more detailed bullet points. For the first one, that was right for me, but we all know that it's much more engaging to watch someone speak card free, but that's another discussion isn't it? Anyway, I was nervous. As in might-vomit-in-front-of-an-audience nervous. It didn't help that the event started in the evening so I had had a day of balancing children and work and life (and I think a Tesco shop) before I left. I had had a series of pep talks from some of my friends, but I was still worried and then I had a thought. What if I did absolutely mess it up? And I mean vomit on stage. Not be able to string a sentence together. Have a panic attack level of mess up. What would actually happen?

I'd look a bit of a fool.

That was literally it. I thought about what was really important, just for a moment. If I made an utter fool of myself, would I not have a job tomorrow? Nope. Would I not have my two little boys and husband at home waiting for me? Nope. Would the car burst into flames to stop me getting home? I mean it might but not because I'd given a crap talk. Everything that really mattered to me would be completely unaffected if I embarrassed myself at the highest level and then it suddenly didn't feel so bad.

I still wanted to do my very best, but it did feel much less terrifying.

I gave the talk – it was good. I mean I don't think any of the greats need to be quaking in their boots over it, but I delivered the talk in the correct time frame, people liked it, I got a laugh or two, the slides worked – it was good. Afterwards I had some lovely comments from the audience which was so nice and that was that.

I decided it must be a fluke so I applied for another, got it and that one was much better. I'll be applying for more too.

Now, that is a fairly long winded way of explaining my first public speaking experience to you, but I felt it was worth a few hundred words because if I can do it, you sure as heck can. Yes, public speaking is scary. It can be really scary. But it's not the most rational fear there is. If you can find a way to handle it, you can do it and share your message with the world.

Why public speaking helps your 'expert status'

As I said, since giving my first TEDx talk, I've been able to get a second (also around the theme of social media but this time more around the power of collaboration), increase the amount of guest lecturing I do, give seminars at industry specific events, chair discussion panels at events, speak on live stages – so much. Whether saying I'd given a TEDx talk helped, I'm not so sure. For some opportunities I would say it did, but for others not so much. But what it did, without a doubt, was give me the confidence to push myself forward as the expert in the area, now with 'proof' to back up the claim. When people list their accolades on their websites, you'll often see places they're connected to, events they've spoken at, work they've had published, etc. Connecting to the right organisations and experiences gives us an alignment with a brand that echoes our own beliefs or helps to elevate our own status in the eyes of those that matter to us as a brand and business and public speaking is a superb way to do this.

Exposure to a new audience

Of course, public speaking doesn't just influence the people who know you – oh no. You get to reach more people. If you speak at somewhere like TEDx, you might have some friends come along and watch, but what you'll more likely get is exposure to a brand new audience. These people will likely come from different backgrounds to your immediate circles, maybe they live close to the location in question, but they're not likely to be your exact niche. Even with more industry specific events, if you walk up there on the stage and give a talk, the audience is unlikely to be made up of 100% of your current fans, followers and contacts and that's amazing. It's brilliant to be able to speak to and work with your current 'tribe', but these people will probably be consuming all the content we have discussed in this book already. For some people, this might be the first contact with you and might encourage them to find out more. Or it might even be a way to get to know the 'lurkers' on your social media who follow you and obviously like what you're doing but you didn't realise until they came up to see you at the end of the talk.

Even if you're quite niche in what you do, you're likely to be able to share stories that connect to different people and make you relatable to them in some way. We're all humans after all and share so many similar character traits. I imagine many of you reading this could relate to something in the story of my first TEDx talk above, right? The actual talk had a strong equestrian link but that doesn't make it any less valuable to anyone else that was reading the above, even if they don't know one end of a horse from the other. Also, don't forget that you never know who is watching these talks, either in real time sat in the audience or online if they're recorded. I have this thing about the power of one, which ties in rather beautifully with Kevin Bacon's six degrees of separation concept between everyone on the earth. You just never know who's watching and even if you do, you don't know who they know.

Video potential

When you speak at events, there's usually the opportunity to have your talk recorded (and by this, I mean a friend with a phone if all else fails), or it might even be recorded as part of the event. With TEDx, the talks get recorded and are then shared to their insanely huge YouTube channel. This might make you want to cringe or go and hide under a rock, but we are our own worse critics. When I watch my first TEDx talk back I can't believe how wild my hair is. I mean, like anyone else in the world is realistically going to click off because my hair's 'too much' for them. But it bothers me and if you watch, I ironed that shirt before my talk but it turns out that the fabric is made to crease and a seatbelt being fastened over it made a LOT of creases. But what having that video out there in the world also does (beyond exposing a fabric that's made to crease, and my crazy hair), is show people that I really do know my stuff. So many people talk a really good game on social media and on their websites, but I think that when you see someone speak and talk on a subject they claim to love and have a deep understanding of, you can really see what the situation is. If you want to do more public speaking, having a showreel of sorts can be really good and having the video 'evidence' can also allow you to repurpose the heck out of a talk.

With a video, if you recorded it (and you were allowed to record at the event) you can do a lot with it. You can upload to YouTube, embed into a blog on your website, make snippets for Facebook/Instagram/TikTok, extract quotes, write a blog about the video or highlighting area – SO much. So, when we look at using our time wisely and making every bit of content we create work hard for us, you have that scope too.

It's free and you might even get paid!

Public speaking has another benefit, you can do it for free or you might even get paid to do it!

I get paid to speak in some situations and speak at others for free depending on the set up of the organisation, the potential exposure and gain and a variety of other elements that get taken into account. I don't pay to speak. Ever. That's not the point for me at all. A bit like writing an article for a magazine. When it comes to speaking, I'm sharing a different take on something, or a specific piece of knowledge that I think will help people, and I'm not paying for that as it should (hopefully) enhance what else is going on at the event.

When we look at ways to grow a business or personal brand on a shoestring, free ways are obviously a great place to focus but I would urge just a little caution here. You don't have to speak at everything you get invited to. Not all opportunities are created equal. When you look at places to speak, think about why you're doing it. In 2018 I pushed myself a little hard and spoke whenever the opportunity appeared, and that was the right thing to do in that situation. It really broke my 'I can't do this' thought process about speaking in public, more because when I thought that I then thought 'oh come on, you've done this LOADS now'. But now I exercise caution even if money is on the table. You need to look at what's to gain from it or what you could possibly gain from it and also the work you're going to need to put in to pull it off AND what you're going to need to do to make up the time has been taken up because of it. Sometimes the balance isn't there. If that's the case, give people enough notice (or don't say yes in the first place) but thank them and ask them to keep you in mind for the future – no one minds. Your direction may have changed by next year and that opportunity may be perfect, so you don't need to burn your bridges when you say no.

Seeing people in person

There's something different when you see someone in person – and that's definitely a plus of public speaking. As I said, some people can talk an exceptional game on social media, but when you scratch the surface there is no substance there. When you speak, there are not that many places to hide. Especially if you throw open the floor to Q and A (and I LOVE doing this as I learn so much from the questions asked and feel like I'm making a difference). But more than that, when you watch someone speak, you get to learn so much more about them. I know when I watch someone give a talk, it's not just the words from their mouth I'm taking in. It's how they're saying it. If I consider working with someone or want to learn more about them/take a course they're running, whatever, I want to KNOW that I'm going to be engaged in how they're putting that content across. If their talk delivery is dry as hell, I'm out. If their manner is rather aloof and superior, they're probably not the person for me. If they speak in jargon to bewilder the audience, I have no interest. See what I mean? If they're quietly confident at the same time as being warm and interested in what's happening in the world, I'm in. I want someone who's been in the trenches and is trying and testing and applying what they say, I don't have a whole lot of time for theory without testing. I can get all this from watching someone do their thing on stage.

Video can also help massively with this, so if you don't have the opportunity to speak on stage for a bit, embrace video even more. I've genuinely had people approach me like we're friends who have known each other for ages and I've no recollection of them. This isn't because I've had a memory fail, it's because they've seen me doing a live on Facebook or watched a YouTube video and know how I am and how I behave and feel more of a connection to me. When you realise you haven't completely forgotten who the person speaking to you is (because, to be clear, you don't actually know them so you can't have forgotten them), this is a really lovely thing and when you think about building a business or brand; how amazing is that? Through using a one-to-many framework, you're making amazing connections with people. Don't underestimate this.

Another benefit of most public speaking 'gigs' is that afterwards, if you stick around, you usually have the opportunity to speak to people (that is, if they want to speak to you!), and I've had some really lovely, interesting chats through this. In this situation, because you've broken down the first wall and let people get to know you, the people who speak to you are genuinely interested in what you have to say and don't feel 'weird' about approaching someone they have never spoken to before, straight out of the blue. This allows you to get much deeper in your conversation at a much faster pace. And that's a real win.

How to get started

There are lots of ways to get started in public speaking, my own route is one, but I also know that my route is far from the most conventional or normal. I think I was probably a little lucky that everything seemed to come together at the right moment and I knew who to contact and just did it. There are some groups on Facebook that look to support people with their public speaking endeavours, and there are many real life groups around the country that can help you.

Top tips for public speaking

All the below are from my own experience and as I type this

I feel ever so slightly like a fraud because I know that I have a long way to go to be the speaker I want to be. But I am genuinely out there doing it, so these tips are ones that have helped me and will hopefully help you embrace speaking to an audience.

1. It isn't as bad as you think. Like with all things we haven't done a lot of, we build it up in our heads to make it absolutely terrifying but it really isn't.
2. Stuff goes wrong and it's absolutely fine. The audience aren't there to see you fail. If your microphone falls off/you trip over/anything else you're scared of happens, it's going to be fine, it can be fixed and you can crack on.
3. Your first time will feel terrifying. When you climb up there, you're going to get the butterflies out in force. It doesn't mean you shouldn't be there or it is going to go wrong. It means you're pushing your comfort zone. Well done.
4. Think of what you have to lose and in most cases it's very little that matters. I still use this tip now when the butterflies kick off and cross the excitement to terror level of flapping. Really, WHAT HAVE YOU GOT TO LOSE?
5. Practice. But also roll with the punches. When I give talks now, I'm much more a roll with the punches kind of girl. I have a plan in my head and sometimes I write a few bullet points down, but I don't over plan. It doesn't work for me. I practice elements in my head when I'm walking the dog quite often. When I gave my TEDx talks, I practiced much more because they have strict time limits and I didn't want to go over.
6. Find what works for you. Some people can memorise talks, some people can't. Some want to and some can't think of anything worse. For me, trying to memorise a talk makes me feel incredibly anxious because I KNOW I will not cover part of it and I also know I'll be distracted by trying to find

the bit I've forgotten in my head and that will likely throw me off. I do very little written prep for talks now which I know would terrify some people, but I probably do more mental prep than most. If I over plan, it backfires, so I don't.

7. Get some cheerleaders and ones who get what you're trying to do. Everyone has their own take on giving talks and that's absolutely fine, but you're not them so you don't need that input. You do need people who will listen, offer helpful pointers, and will be there saying 'you've got this' when you don't think you can.

8. Not everyone needs to understand why you're doing it. Not everyone needs to know where you're speaking. I remember feeling a little gutted when someone very close to me had no idea what TEDx, or TED, was because I felt it would be a really great thing and I was excited and they asked me if it was connected to teacher education days. But the thing was, TED and TEDx weren't and aren't in their world so why would they? But what's true is that it doesn't matter if no one but you sees the value in what you're doing. Sometimes you really do have to be your own hero.

9. Breathe. Speak slower than you think you should. Record yourself and listen back if you want to confirm your speed and breaths. When we get nervous we can talk much faster and hold our breath. You don't want to be doing either of these things.

10. Enjoy. Yes, enjoy the experience, every bit of it. You'll learn so much and in one way or another it will be helping you and your personal brand/business.

14. Bye For Now

Well, I can't quite believe we're here so soon. I want to say if you have got this far then please accept a virtual kiss and hug from me and if you've been sharing your progress on social and tagging me, accept a virtual drink too – I appreciate it all.

I've always wanted to write a book. I enjoy writing and sharing things with people and I LOVE it when people put the ideas and tactics shared into action and I see the change I know is possible. I get far more of a kick from people I care about doing well than I do from my own successes. Being able to share what I see as the blueprint for success for a personal brand or business on a tight budget has been such a lovely experience but the next bit is the most exciting for me, I mean, what are YOU going to do with what you've read? How are you going to grow your business or personal brand without dipping into your gin/chocolate/jewellery/shoe money? Or more realistically, how are you going to do it in a way that will allow you to put the money you make back into the business and allow you to invest in bigger and better systems that will take your business or brand to the next level. How exciting it that?

I would LOVE to hear how you're getting on and whether you'd like to join my Small & Supercharged™ Facebook Group, tag me on social media (I'm @rheafreemanpr on Instagram and Rhea Freeman on Facebook) when you're putting some of the tips from these pages into practice, pop on over and follow me on Facebook or Instagram and DM me with what you're doing. I would love to hear from you, I really would.

You can also find out more about my membership group, Small & Supercharged™ Mastermind[1] if you're keen to join the most incredible community of lovely people who really are going places.

So, thank you, you go getter you. Don't hide all the amazing stuff you have to give the world and don't use a tight budget as the reason not to get out there and shine as bright as you can. People need you and what you have to offer and it's your duty to share it.

Notes

1. https://www.facebook.com/groups/smallandsuperchargedmastermind

About the Author

Rhea Freeman is an award winning PR adviser, Meta Lead Trainer, #SheMeansBusiness accredited trainer, 2 x TEDx speaker, award winning podcaster, and small business coach who has created a name for herself in helping brands promote themselves on really tight or non-existent budgets.

Her first appearance in the world of PR was over 15 years ago when copywriting led her into preparing editorial copy for magazines for clients and things snowballed from there! Along the way, Rhea has worked in-house as a Marketing Manager and, in a freelance capacity, has advised a large number of businesses from sole traders through to SMEs. She has really carved a niche for herself in terms of capitalising on the free opportunities offered to brands to promote themselves better, whatever their budget.

As social media began to increase and impact the potential reach of printed media a good few years ago, Rhea set about learning all she could about this 'new' world and started working to educate her clients on the benefits of the relevant platforms and how these could help their businesses. Fast forward a good few years and now Rhea spends a lot of time teaching people how to utilise social media for their businesses, teaching the skills relevant to each platform alongside traditional PR. She helps them to understand how to work with influencers and brand ambassadors, how to create better content, grow mailing lists and learn how to market a business well with whatever budget is available.

In addition to working with small businesses, Rhea also guest lectures at two universities and supports associations and federations in the education of their members. She also writes for a number of publications on the subjects of social media, PR and marketing, enjoys public speaking and has given two TEDx talks and spoken at numerous events. She chats about social media and small business on local radio whenever she can and also runs a free Facebook group called Small & Supercharged™ to help people in her industry connect and a membership group of the same name… but with Mastermind on the end.

In short, she's a self proclaimed geek. And you'll find her hanging about on social media more than she'd freely admit. Find her @rheafreemanpr on Instagram, /RheaFreemanPR on Facebook and @rheafreeman on Twitter.

Aside from this, Rhea is a mum of twin boys, a dog mum and a horse mum. She lives in Worcestershire with her husband and two and four legged family members.

Printed in Great Britain
by Amazon

84213868R00104